D0097568

HOW TO FEEL GOOD

HOW TO FEEL GOOD

20 THINGS TEENS CAN DO

BY TRICIA MANGAN, MA

Magination Press • Washington, DC
American Psychological Association

Published by
MAGINATION PRESS
An Educational Publishing Foundation Book
American Psychological Association
750 First Street, NE
Washington, DC 20002

For more information about our books, including a complete catalog, please write to us, call 1-800-374-2721, or visit our website at www.apa.com/pubs/magination.

Book design by Naylor Design, Inc., Washington, DC
Printed by Sheridan Books, Inc., Ann Arbor, MI

Library of Congress Cataloging-in-Publication Data is available
LCCN: 2011 020 623
ISBN-10: 1-4338-1041-7
ISBN-13: 978-1-4338-1041-1

Manufactured in the United States of America
10 9 8 7 6 5 4 3 2 1

CONTENTS

DEAR READER

We all would like to feel good, right? But what does "feeling good" actually mean? How do you know when you're feeling good? Take a moment to notice how you're feeling right now. Are you calm? Irritable? Sad? Maybe you're not exactly sure what you're feeling. Why is it so important to feel good, anyway? How does it affect you if you don't feel good? If you aren't sure how to answer these questions, you're not alone. We may all want to feel good, but understanding how to do that—especially during difficult times—can be confusing.

How to Feel Good: 20 Things Teens Can Do will help you understand what feeling good is all about. It will show you how to feel good by teaching you the skills to stay calm and self-confident when problems arise. This book provides you with lots of tools to help you feel good. But don't worry—you don't have to learn them all at once. Although you can read every section in order, this book is designed so that you can skip around and do one section at a time, focusing on the tools you think are most useful for you right now.

Inside, you will find out how to overcome frustration and develop patience so that you can achieve your goals. You will learn that your mind and your body work in unison—what one experiences, so does the other. So, to feel good, it's important to be kind to your *whole* self by treating your body and mind with kindness. You will also discover that feeling good sometimes involves turning your attention away from yourself and toward other people. Learning to put yourself in someone else's shoes and see things from their perspective can help you develop compassion and make it easier to forgive.

You will also discover what an important role your thoughts play in how you feel. Many times, we are unaware of what we're thinking. Our inner voice whispers just loudly enough for the messages it sends to go through but, unless we pay close attention, we don't hear them. Without knowing, we might think negative things about ourselves that get in the way of feeling good. This book will teach you to tune in to your inner voice and replace any negative messages with more positive ones.

The truth is, you have a very special power. Although you can't always control what happens to you or what other people say and do, you can control what *you* do when difficult situations arise. And learning to respond in healthy ways to tough situations can help you feel good about yourself and your world. If you master the skills described in this book, you will be more likely to reach your goals in life, to be sensitive to the feelings and needs of others, to be confident in social situations, and to bounce back more easily from mistakes.

Are you ready to discover how powerful you are?

HAVE A
POSITIVE
ATTITUDE

Did you know that what you think changes how you feel and act?

Imagine you are an astronaut on a mission. Your mission is to keep yourself healthy, happy, and strong while you are out exploring the universe. Astronauts get commands from Mission Control to help them complete their mission safely. Your mind is just like Mission Control. Every message you send from your head tells your body how to behave. That means if you let unhelpful messages take over the control room, you may go off course. Your mission to feel good could get sidetracked.

Everyone has unhelpful thoughts sometimes. A voice in your head might say things like, "I can't do this," or, "I'll never be good enough, so there's no point in trying." If you let that voice say those things over and over, you might start to believe they're true. Then, your body hears those messages and does just what it's told.

But you have the power to keep that from happening. You can change your attitude by replacing the unhelpful messages with helpful ones. Let's say your mind sometimes tells you "Nobody cares about me." Think of examples to prove that voice wrong, like: "That's not true. My teacher cares so much about how well I do in school that she spent one-on-one time with me in class to help me. And my mom gave me a big hug this morning—she wouldn't have done that if she didn't care."

The Importance of Attitude: A + B = C

It's not the things that happen in our lives that cause us to feel one way or another—it's how we *think* about these events that determines how we feel.

There's an easy equation to help you remember this important point: A + B = C

A stands for *activating event*. An activating event is simply something that happens in your life. Examples of these situations may include going to the doctor, performing in a recital in front of a large audience, switching schools, or trying out for a sports team.

B stands for *beliefs*. Beliefs are personal. They are the thoughts you have about yourself, your friends and family, and the world around you. Beliefs contribute to your feelings and actions (C) to a particular event (A).

C stands for *consequences*. These consequences come in the form of unhelpful emotions—such as anxiety, frustration, anger, or sadness—or actions that you take. This is a direct result of what you believe (B) or think about the event (A).

> We all have different experiences as we grow up, and those experiences influence our beliefs in different ways.

It's important to remember that your beliefs aren't necessarily the same as someone else's. That's because we all have different experiences as we grow up, and those experiences influence our beliefs in different ways. Sometimes, situations that other kids don't think are a big deal can lead us to have some tough emotions because they trigger unpleasant beliefs we have about ourselves. For example, let's say you get invited to a birthday party by a classmate you don't know well. Others who received an invitation appear to be really happy and excited about the party. However, you are worried and nervous. In your mind, you think, "I should be happy about being invited. I guess there's something wrong with me." You also think, "I can never make friends with people. Any time I try to say something, I sound stupid. I don't know why he would invite someone like me."

One of the best ways to help yourself overcome negative automatic beliefs is to challenge them with more realistic, positive ones. For example, challenge the thought, "I never know what to say around kids I don't know," by telling yourself, "Actually, sometimes I do say things to kids I don't know, and sometimes they answer me back."

A + B = C, but we can add two more letters to the equation.

D stands for *disputing irrational beliefs.* To challenge your self-defeating beliefs, ask yourself a few questions:

* Is this belief logical? Does it even make sense?

✳ Do I have any proof that this belief is actually true?
  Where's the evidence?

✳ Is this belief useful at all? Does it help me in any way?

E stands for the *effects* of changing your beliefs. Did thinking
more positively cause your anxiety to lessen? Has your anger
or frustration gone away?

Astronaut ABCs

While out on a mission, an astronaut usually keeps in close
contact with Mission Control. Communications satellites
stationed in space help members of Mission Control talk to
astronauts using radio or TV waves. Sometimes, bad storms
can affect the satellites and interfere with communication.

Imagine this situation (A): Our astronaut gets a garbled message from Mission Control. He tries to respond, but his message
doesn't go through. All communication lines go silent. Almost
immediately, he starts panicking. He becomes very anxious. His
heart rate speeds up, he starts shaking a little bit, and he feels
light-headed and sick to his stomach. He automatically thinks
(B) to himself, "I *must* complete this mission, and I can't do it
without Mission Control. I'll disappoint the world if I don't
accomplish this. Why do bad things *always* seem to happen
to me?" The more the astronaut thinks about it, the more
anxious he becomes (C).

How could the astronaut handle that same situation in a
different way—one in which he helps himself to feel better?
Imagine the same situation (A) with different beliefs (B): Once
again, the astronaut receives the garbled message and then all
communications stop. He recognizes that he's starting to get
anxious because he feels the palms of his hands getting sweaty
and his heart rate speeding up. As soon as he notices these

physical cues, he takes a deep breath in and exhales slowly.
He does this a few times to help slow down his heart rate and
relax himself. As he continues to breathe slowly and deeply,
he realizes that his automatic beliefs about the situation were
negative. He worried that he would never regain contact and
didn't believe in his own abilities to accomplish his mission
without guidance from Mission Control. So he disputes those
thoughts with more positive ones. "I have trained for many years
to be an astronaut, and I am well prepared to handle this situation," he thinks. He also thinks, "I know storms can temporarily
interfere with the satellites, so I am sure that communication will
go back to normal once the storm passes." After modifying his
thoughts and controlling his breathing, the sweat on his palms
starts to dry and his heart rate slows down. He continues to
reassure himself by repeating those positive thoughts in his head
as often as he needs to keep himself composed.

Work on Your ABCs

First, make the connection between your thoughts and feelings. Think of a time when your thoughts and beliefs about a
situation led you to feel good. Label the A, B, and C of that
situation.

EXAMPLE:
A = Pop quiz
B = "I've paid attention in class and done all the homework, so even
    if there are a few things I don't know, I should do pretty well."
C = Feeling calm, relaxed, and self-confident

Then, figure out what you were thinking during a harder
situation. Identify a recent event (A) that resulted in you
experiencing an uncomfortable emotion (C) like sadness,
frustration, anger, or anxiety. Label the A and C. Then fill in B

by figuring out what unhelpful thoughts may have led you to feel uncomfortable.

Sing Away the Unhelpful Bs

Think of an unhelpful or unwelcome thought (B) that comes into your mind a lot. Come up with as many helpful thoughts as you can to dispute that thought. For example, let's say you often think, "I'm not talented enough to win anything." Some helpful thoughts to dispute that would include, "Working hard and learning from past mistakes is what makes a person talented—not winning," or, "Lots of really talented people don't win. Not everybody can win every time."

Make a song verse out of your list of helpful thoughts. You can put them to a tune you already know or come up with your own. Sing the song to yourself every day and every time the unhelpful beliefs pop into your mind.

SHINE A SPOTLIGHT ON GOOD THINGS

Every day, there are lots of things happening in your world. In just one day, some good things might happen (the sun could be shining or you might get a good grade on a test) and some not-so-good things might happen (you could fall off your bike or get in trouble).

When one or two things go wrong, it can seem like the light has gone out on all the good things. That can make you feel dark and gloomy. Everything in your whole life seems bad. But it's not that the good things aren't there. It's just that you've stopped paying attention to them. It's as if you took a spotlight and turned it away from the good things and onto the bad ones. This is called *selective attention*. Selective attention is when you focus your awareness only on certain things and ignore all others. When we pick out all the not-so-good things going on around us, our view of the world is similarly not so good.

When one or two things go wrong, it can seem like the light has gone out on all the good things.

Instead, try to pay attention to what you want your world to be. When you can, turn that spotlight (your attention) away from the bad things and light your world back up.

To really shift the spotlight, change your focus, and feel good, you need to make sure the positive thoughts outnumber the negative ones. To do that, try something called *savoring*. Savoring means taking the time to focus on and appreciate something. You can savor memories from the past or anticipate something enjoyable you're going to do soon in the future. Close your eyes and imagine something pleasant. When you savor something, the memories or thoughts of that event can make your whole body feel better.

But it's also important to savor things happening in your life right now, in this moment. And don't just focus on the big things—there are many small things that bring us pleasure every day that we overlook because we're in a rush or too busy thinking about something else. For example, do you like reading books? The next time you open up a book, take the time to notice what is so wonderful about the book. Feel the pages— are they smooth or worn? Open up the book and take a sniff— does it have a distinct smell? Does the book binding or cover crackle when you open it? What appeals to you about the artwork on the cover?

No matter how much you try to focus your attention on positive things, there may be times when you can't just ignore a difficult problem. Unhelpful thoughts about that situation may keep coming into your mind in spite of your efforts. Reframing is one way to deal with a difficult situation. *Reframing* involves finding a new way to think about a situation so that it doesn't upset you so much.

Each of us looks at a situation through a certain frame of mind. Remember that A + B = C from *1. Have a Positive Attitude (pg. 9):* How we feel (C) about an event (A) is influenced by our thoughts and beliefs (B). Our view of the situation is colored by our unhelpful beliefs. You can change the way a problem looks by changing your frame of mind—that is, by changing the way you think about it.

Imagine there is a framed painting on the wall in the hallway outside of your room. The art piece has always frightened you, and lately the thought of it outside your door is keeping you up at night. You are frightened and anxious (C) because you believe the animals in the painting are out to get you. But you decide to challenge that thought by asking yourself, "Is that really logical? Could animals really come out of a painting and get me?" You remind yourself every night when those unhelpful thoughts arise that animals cannot come out of a painting, and after a little time, you start to be less worried. During the daytime, you get closer to the painting and look at it. The more you look at it, the less scared you are when you realize the animals aren't moving and you are still safe. Nothing physically changed about the painting, but it appears that way to you. You didn't have to throw the piece of art away or avoid the hallway outside your door. You just had to try to see it through a different frame of mind.

Light Up Your World

Stop giving the bad things the stage, and shine a spotlight on the good ones. Turn your selective attention toward the positive and name at least three good things that happened to you today.

Savor the Good Things

Step 1: Identify events or situations that make you feel good, that have made you feel good in the past, or that you anticipate will make you feel good in the future. Think about big milestones like birthdays or vacations, as well as smaller day-to-day events like eating ice cream or playing with your pet.

Here are a few other ideas to help you:

* Making new friends
* Taking a trip to a zoo, museum, or other interesting place
* Accomplishing something positive at school
* Accomplishing something positive at home or with your family
* Finishing a book
* Smelling flowers

Step 2: Close your eyes and imagine each of those situations. Let your mind bring up all the details of the event. Try only to focus on this one thing. It's normal if other thoughts come into your mind—for example, thoughts of something that upset you or something you're worried about or just thoughts about what you have to do tomorrow. Whenever those thoughts come into your mind, tell yourself that it's ok and try to let them go and re-focus on the positive experience you're savoring.

Step 3: Try to savor something every day for five minutes.

Adopt a Different Frame of Mind

Identify something that you have a hard time thinking about in a positive way. Try to see an obstacle as an exciting adventure, or think about a personal weakness as an opportunity to develop your skills. Certain words are clues that let you know you should reframe your attitude—words like "never," "always," "must," "horrible," or "worst." Don't be so absolute— reframe using words like "sometimes" or "not so bad." Sometimes it's also good not to take things so personally. Reframe by thinking of another explanation that doesn't focus the blame on you. Use the examples below to help you.

Original Attitude: "I can never pass spelling tests."

Reframed Attitude: "Spelling is tough for me, but I have sometimes done well on spelling tests. If I review the words over and over again, I will get better and better at spelling them."

Original Attitude: "I'm moving on to a higher grade and have to switch schools. I won't be able to make friends. This is going to be awful."

Reframed Attitude: "Actually, starting at a new school might not be so bad. It could be really fun because this school has sports teams and after-school activities my old school didn't have. I might make friends soon."

No matter how much you try to focus your attention on positive things, there may be times when you can't just ignore a difficult problem.

Original Attitude: "Susan didn't say hello to me at lunch. She must hate me."

Reframed Attitude: "Susan might have been having a bad day and wasn't in the mood to talk. It probably has nothing to do with me."

COMPARE TO NO ONE—YOU ARE AN ORIGINAL

Have you ever drawn a picture and felt really proud of it until you saw someone else's picture and thought theirs was much better? Or maybe you were really excited after you scored a goal in your soccer game...until your friend scored two goals.

When you compare yourself to other people, you can make yourself think you're not good enough. You never seem to be the tallest student, or the one with the most friends, or the funniest or smartest kid in your class. It can start to seem like people are outshining you in everything you do. Kids who compare themselves to others are less likely to feel good about themselves. That's because when you look at other people, you're often focusing your attention on what makes them better than you. When we're unsure of how we're doing, we look around to find examples of other people who are doing "better." That strategy is certain to leave you feeling disappointed in yourself.

You don't have to be better than anyone to be good enough. There is nobody like you in the whole universe. Everything about you is special and unique.

You don't have to be better than anyone to be good enough. There is nobody like you in the whole universe. Everything about you is special and unique. Nobody draws like you, rides a bicycle like you, or has handwriting quite like yours. Without you, the world would be a different place because being who you are makes a difference to other people.

Not only do you not have to be better than anyone else, you also don't have to win to prove you're good enough. Lots of talented people who work really hard don't win every competition or race. Striving to do the best you can at whatever you do and focusing on enjoying each moment rather than winning or being the best will help you be self-confident and secure.

Everyone has a turn to shine the brightest, including you. But whether you win or lose, you are always an original. And that is good.

Take a Turn and Shine

Think of a time you shined. How did you feel? Were your friends happy for you? Would they want you to be happy for them when they shine? Think of a time when your friends shined. What did you say to them? If you didn't say anything, what could you have said?

Describe How You Shine

Name three ways you are different from anyone else in the world. Explain how those three things have made a difference in the world. For example, maybe one of the things that makes you special is that you are funny and are a great joke-teller. You have made a difference by making others laugh.

Shine Without Winning

Think of someone you admire—for example, a famous athlete, singer, or actor. Describe a time when this person didn't win. Maybe the musician was nominated for a Grammy Award but lost to another musical artist. Does not winning mean they're not good enough? Describe what makes this person shine in spite of losing.

DISCOVER WHAT YOU CAN DO

You are unique. You have important talents that you can develop. You can make the world a better place. Maybe you will grow up and create works of art that inspire people. Or maybe you will be a doctor and help sick people get healthy. Maybe you have a knack for entertaining people, or protecting people, or running a business that makes things like clothes or shoes or other products people need.

You will feel your best when you do things that you enjoy doing. To figure out what those things are, you have to pay close attention. What are you good at doing? What activities do you love so much that you get lost in them and could do them for hours? What are the special skills you show while you're doing those tasks? Once you know what you're good at, you can start looking for other activities that use those same skills. For example, maybe you are an excellent reader and like to spend most of your free time devouring new books. That means you probably have good language skills. With good language skills, you could become a teacher, a lawyer, a fiction or non-fiction writer, a poet, a screenwriter for films, or an editor at a publishing company. You could expand on your interest in language by learning foreign languages or sign language. Or, if the dramatic storytelling of books interests you even more than the language itself, you could explore working in a theater or acting. As another example, let's say that you love putting puzzles together. That means you have good hand–eye coordination and problem-solving skills, and you're also good at recognizing and matching colors and shapes. With those skills, you might also enjoy and be good at graphic design, architecture, or interior design. You may also enjoy building model toys—like cars, airplanes, or houses—or creating sculptural art pieces.

It is likely that you have talents you don't even know about yet. That's why it's important to try new things. Even if you don't like everything you try, you will have learned something about yourself by doing new things. Maybe you think being a pastry chef would be a neat thing to become, but after baking cookies a few times you realize you don't really like it so much. That's OK. By trying your hand at baking, you proved to yourself that you can do new things, and you learned a lot about yourself in the process. You would never have known that you don't love baking if you hadn't tried.

Don't Let Self-Doubt Defeat Discovery

Have you ever said or thought things like, "I can't do anything right," or "I'm not good at anything"? The idea of trying new things can be scary if we've had some negative experiences in the past. We may also be fearful of trying new things if we expect too much of ourselves. Do you believe you have to be the best at everything? Is anything less than perfect unacceptable to you?

Telling yourself that you *must* do everything right, even the first time you try it, only sets you up to be disappointed in yourself. Nobody does everything right the first time or every time. Messing up doesn't make you a failure—it makes you human. Everybody messes up. Instead of looking at mistakes as failures, why not *reframe* them? Mistakes are actually just lessons that point out to you a better way to do something. If it weren't for mistakes, you'd never get better. So mistakes are actually a good thing. They help you develop your special skills. Here are a few tips to follow when trying new things.

Set reasonable expectations. Believe in yourself and expect yourself to have fun when discovering new things. But rather than setting a standard of perfection, allow yourself to try things without evaluating your performance. Don't label your performance as "good" or "bad," and don't compare yourself to others or worry about whether you're doing something "best." Just focus on the enjoyment of learning something new and remind yourself that your skills will develop over time.

Set bite-sized goals. Let's say you decide to try writing poetry. You set a goal to finish a one-page poem every day for a week. On the third day, you have some trouble coming up with an

> You will feel your best when you do things that you enjoy doing. To figure out what those things are, you have to pay close attention.

idea. You spend a lot of time working on it, but can't finish the poem that day. Because you didn't finish, you beat yourself up about it and tell yourself that you've failed. Because of your frustration, you decide to quit writing poetry. Instead of setting such a big goal, why not start smaller? Commit to writing one verse of a poem per day, or one poem per week. If you end up writing more than that, you're ahead of schedule. By setting reasonable goals, you are more likely to succeed and less likely to be frustrated.

Challenge your unhelpful beliefs (B). Remember A + B = C from *1. Have a Positive Attitude (pg. 9)*? If you are experiencing negative consequences (C) like frustration or anxiety when trying new things, identify the negative thoughts (B) that are stopping you from discovering or developing your skills. Work to modify those unhelpful beliefs by challenging them with evidence that you are good at a lot of things.

Give it a chance. Of course you won't love everything you try. But if you give up on something before giving yourself time to fully experience it, you may miss out. What if you gave up on playing musical instruments after a few challenging trumpet lessons? If you tried playing jazz music instead of classical, would you like playing the trumpet more? Is there another instrument you might enjoy more? Give it a chance, and you will find out.

Don't label your performance as "good" or "bad," and don't compare yourself to others or worry about whether you're doing something "best."

Notice You

Take a moment to notice what you like to do. Make a list of some things that you like to do or that you are good at doing. What skills do you use when doing those tasks? Think of some related activities you could try that use those same skills.

Discover What You Can Do

Reach out for help from adults who have jobs or special skills in science, literature, theater, mathematics, politics, the arts, and beyond. Work with a parent, guardian, or teacher to identify professionals who can come to your school or another community location to teach you about their fields of expertise. Alternatively, you might ask to shadow someone at work for part of the day.

Ask About Your Strengths

Sometimes, other people can see strengths in us that we have trouble seeing ourselves. Ask your parents, friends, teachers, or other family members what they believe your strongest characteristics are.

Conquer Self-Doubt

Are there things you'd like to try but haven't done because you think you won't be able to? Write down the name of the activity and the unhelpful thoughts you have associated with it, like, "I'm no good at anything," or, "I always mess up stuff like that." Then challenge those negative beliefs. You might also try asking yourself, "What's the worst that can happen if I try this new thing? Is that consequence really so bad?"

MAKE FRIENDS
WITH YOUR
FEELINGS

Poor feelings. They can have a really hard time making
friends. They sometimes get shoved under the bed
when people don't recognize what they are or know
what to do about them. And that's unfair to them because
they're just trying to tell you something. Like good friends,
feelings are looking out for you. Feelings try to let you know
that something has happened to make you react a certain way,
and that you will better understand what is going on if you
take time to notice them.

It's easy to understand why we might be afraid to come
face-to-face with our emotions at times. They can be confusing. Some emotions—like frustration and anger, or worry and
fear—look and feel so similar that we may have a hard time
figuring out the difference between them. Other times, the
message we're getting from our emotions isn't clear. We might
know that we feel upset, or that we "just don't feel good," but

we can't tell what specific emotion—like anger or sadness—
we're really experiencing.

Then there are times when we know we are angry or sad,
but we're afraid that if we let those emotions out, we might
hurt someone we care about. Or, we may not know how to
handle the emotion, so we try to keep it buried inside. Imagine
that a good friend is worried about you and keeps trying to
warn you about something. Scared that she might tell you
something you don't know how to handle, you shut your door
to keep her out. Because your friend cares about you so much,
she keeps knocking on the door and won't leave until you
listen to her. But you keep holding tight to the doorknob to
make sure she doesn't get in. After a while, you are exhausted
from holding the door to keep her out. Something similar can
happen when you try to keep certain emotions that seem too
big under the bed. It takes a lot of effort to keep emotions
hidden. It can leave you tired and overwhelmed.

But that doesn't have to happen if you choose to make
friends with your feelings. Here are a few tips to help get your
friendship off to a great start.

Learn their names. It's hard to be friends if you don't know
their names, right? And in the case of emotions, there are a lot
of names to learn. There's fear, frustration, jealousy, guilt,
worry, sadness, and a lot more. It will take you some time to
learn them all, so don't fret if you can't distinguish them all
right away.

One good way to start identifying emotions is to examine
facial expressions. Open up an illustrated book and look at the
characters' faces. What do you think they are experiencing?
You could also draw your own faces to show what each
emotion may look like. For example, an angry face may have

scrunched eyebrows and a wide-open mouth (as if it's yelling), whereas an embarrassed face may have eyes that look downward and blushing cheeks.

Pay close attention to how each emotion feels. Once you know their names, get to know your emotions even better by paying closer attention to how they make you feel. Also take note of what types of situations tend to bring them out from beneath the bed. For example, maybe frustration comes out a lot whenever you do homework. When frustration arises, how does it feel? Do you experience pressure in your head? Does your face get red? Do your palms get sweaty? Does your heart beat fast? The earlier you recognize the appearance of these emotions, the earlier you can take action to calm yourself down and feel better.

Remember that it's normal. Everyone experiences difficult emotions—you're not alone. Frustration, anger, and sadness are emotions that we all experience as human beings. Sometimes we may think, "What is wrong with me? Why am I acting this way?" We may look around and think that everyone else seems happy and fine. But the truth is, there's nothing wrong with you. And people who seem fine may be just as uncomfortable as you are under the surface. They may just not want to show it. Or, they may have figured out how to react comfortably to an uncomfortable situation. When things get

Sometimes, the messages we're getting from our emotions aren't clear.

If you ever do have a hard time getting a difficult emotion to go away, ask for help from your mom, your dad, or an adult at school who can help you.

tough, it's important to remind yourself that dealing with difficult emotions sometimes is a normal part of life.

Know that emotions come and go. When you're feeling an uncomfortable emotion, it can seem like it lasts forever. But, in most cases, emotions tend to come and go. For example, you may be upset about a bad grade or an argument with a friend, but after a while your hurt and sadness lessen and you start to feel better. The key is to learn how to cope when the unhelpful emotions do emerge from under the bed. If you can hang in there, remind yourself that this is just temporary, and practice soothing yourself by doing some of the exercises listed at the end of this section, you'll be much better prepared to make it through the tough times. If you ever do have a hard time getting a difficult emotion to go away, ask for help from your mom, your dad, or an adult at school who can help you.

Communication is key. Learning how to communicate your emotions to other people can empower you. The people in your life may not know when you are unhappy, but if you find an appropriate way to tell them, you may feel better just getting your emotion out in the open. Imagine you have been angry with a friend for days because he teased you in front of several of your classmates, and they all laughed. The anger eats at you all day when you're at school. When you go home after school, you're in such a bad mood that you pick fights with your sister and talk back to your mom. Your family is upset with your behavior, and you think you're just totally alone. But your family doesn't know why you suddenly started acting this way, and you wouldn't have to cope with these tough emotions alone if you got up the courage to talk to them about it.

Talking about your emotions isn't always easy. You may have trouble finding the right words, or you may worry that the person you tell won't be supportive of you. That's why it's best to start by telling someone you trust—like your parents, a teacher, or the school counselor—what's going on and how a situation is making you feel. Then, they can show you how to talk about how you feel, and also how to talk about what you need to feel better.

Find positive role models. Watching how other people deal with their emotions in difficult situations can teach you a lot. For example, have you ever watched your teacher stay calm and bring the class back to order when it gets a little out of hand sometimes? What emotions do you think she feels when that happens? How does she react? What does she say and do to handle the situation effectively, and how might you apply that to your own life?

Get to Know Emotions

Below are two lists: One is a list of emotions and the other is a list of experiences that commonly happen in peoples' lives.

a) For each emotion, think of a personal situation you've been through and the feeling that resulted from that situation.

b) For each event, select one emotion, or more, that you experienced or felt during that event or personal situation.

Emotions

Embarrassment	✳	Guilt
Shame	✳	Anxiety
Fear	✳	Disgust
Loneliness	✳	Sadness
Grief	✳	Happiness
Envy	✳	Love
Annoyance	✳	Anger
Hurt	✳	Disappointment
Despair	✳	Worry
Helplessness	✳	Powerlessness
Frustration	✳	Excitement
Delight	✳	Trust
Courage	✳	Satisfaction
Calm	✳	Relief
Surprise	✳	Doubt
Jealousy	✳	Hopefulness
Joy	✳	Pride

Events

Death of a close friend or family member
Death of a pet
Argument with a friend
Argument with a family member
Getting in trouble at school
Getting bullied
Winning an award
Making a new friend
Having a friend saying something mean to you or about you
Parents getting a divorce
Doing really well on your report card
Scoring a soccer goal
Having a friend say something nice to you or about you

Clean Out From Under Your Bed

Staying in touch with your emotions every day can help keep them from piling up and becoming overwhelming.

Journaling. One way to communicate with your emotions is to keep a journal. In your journal, write down the emotions, feelings, and thoughts you have each day. If you're not sure what is causing you to feel a certain way, that's OK too. Just describe what you feel as best you can and see if you can figure out what happened that made you feel that way.

Drawing. Sometimes it can be hard to describe in words how we feel. Instead of journaling, try drawing a picture of something you felt upset about this week. Share your drawing or journal pages with a loved one. Work together to find the words for your emotion and how you were feeling. Did drawing and talking about things help you understand?

Stay One Step Ahead of Your Emotions

The key to keeping your emotions under control is to pay close attention to them. Although you may not recognize frustration, anxiety, or anger at first, you may notice yourself feeling uncomfortable. That's your cue to take action. By acting on feelings when they first start to appear, you can prevent them from getting to big or overwhelming. First, identify how the emotion affects your body. Are your back and shoulder muscles tense? Are you sick to your stomach? Are your cheeks red? Next, create a plan of action for how to cope with difficult emotions when they arise. Depending on where you are, certain plans may not be appropriate. For example, if you're in class, you might not just be able to get up and leave, so it's a

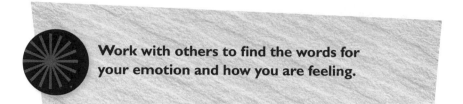

Work with others to find the words for your emotion and how you are feeling.

good idea to come up with a Plan B. You can see an example in the chart below. As shown in the example, you may decide that any time you start to become angry, you will take a "time-out" and remove yourself from the situation so that you can give yourself a chance to calm down. During the time-out, you will close your eyes and breathe deeply and slowly in and out. You may also imagine something peaceful, like the beach or a forest, or you can think of a memory that makes you feel good. If you can't remove yourself from the situation, you can go to Plan B and just do the deep breathing and imagination work until you feel calmer.

Emotion	Things to Notice	Plan A	Plan B
Anger	Pressure or ache in my head, tension in my stomach, feeling hot and red in the face	Take a time-out and walk away. During the time-out, breathe deeply or imagine something relaxing or positive.	Close my eyes or look at a fixed point and block out what is making me angry. Breathe deeply and imagine something relaxing until I feel calmer.

Prepare Yourself

One way to get more comfortable with talking about your emotions is to act out or role-play situations where difficult feelings might arise. Think of something you are facing in the future that makes you anxious or worried. Maybe you're anticipating seeing someone at school who you previously had an argument with, or maybe you have to give a presentation to the class and are worried about being embarrassed or making a mistake. Being able to rehearse and come up with a script for what to say can help to reduce anxiety and make you prepared to deal with difficult situations and emotions. Working with a parent, teacher, or counselor, practice what you could say in the situation you're anticipating. Practice as often as you need to until you start to feel more comfortable.

LIVE IN THE PRESENT

Take a few slow, deep breaths. What's happening right now, in this moment? What do you hear? What do you see? What are your fingers touching? Can you smell any scents in the air?

Maybe you didn't even notice some of those things until you started paying attention to them. It's easy to tune out what is happening in the present because we get lost in our heads. We sometimes spend a lot of time thinking about something that happened in the past—like a mistake we made or a hurtful thing someone said about us. Or sometimes we worry about the future—about a test that is coming up in school or about what might happen the next time we see a classmate who was mean to us.

The problem with living in the past is that we can't change it. It has already happened, so we can't go back and re-do it a different way. It's good to learn from our past mistakes and try

> **Instead of wasting the day worrying about tomorrow, what if, instead, you kept your mind totally focused on all the important things that are going on today?**

to do better next time, but spending too much time dwelling on something that happened doesn't help us on our mission to feel good.

Just like you can't change the past, you also can't control the future. Thinking too much about tomorrow's spelling test won't make you do better. In fact, it will probably just make you really nervous, so you might do worse. Instead of wasting the day worrying about tomorrow, what if, instead, you kept your mind totally focused on all the important things that are going on today? Focusing your attention totally on what's happening in the present is called *mindfulness*. Practicing mindfulness can benefit your mental and physical well-being. First, it relieves stress. By focusing only on what's happening now, you stop worrying about what happened before or what will happen in the future. That calms you down. Second, by reducing tension, mindfulness exercises can improve your mood, help you sleep better, soothe your nervous stomach, and reduce any aches and pains. Learning how to be mindful will give you the power to make yourself feel good.

Make a Change to a Routine

We all develop habits or routines—things we do the same way practically every day. Brushing your teeth and tying your shoes are examples of routine behaviors. We do these things so often that we sometimes zone out and do them mindlessly. Practice being mindful by changing the way you complete these routines. For example, if you usually put your right shoe on and then your left, try putting on your left shoe and then your right. Or, if you are used to putting on your shoes before your coat, try putting on your coat first and leaving your shoes for last. These changes will make you wake up and pay attention because you're not used to doing things in this new way. As you complete each task, use your senses to experience what you're doing. Make note of how the fabric of the shoelaces feels—is it rough and textured, or soft and worn? Feel the weight of the coat fabric pulling across your shoulders as you bend down to put on your shoes. Notice the mud stain on the sole of your shoe. Listen to the sound of the rubber sole squeaking on the floor as you wiggle your foot to slide it in.

Live in the Present

Practice living in the present moment. List three things you notice that are happening right now. Use your five senses— sight, hearing, taste, touch, and smell—to help you. Can you see a spider crawling on the wall? Can you hear a bird chirping? Can you taste chocolate in your mouth from a cookie you ate earlier? Can you smell dinner cooking? Do your fingers feel sticky or soft and clean?

Remind Yourself

To keep your mind from wandering off to the past or future, it can be helpful to find something that will remind you to come back to the present. For example, you might choose to wear a bracelet or attach a keychain to your school backpack. Every time you see the bracelet or keychain, stop what you are doing and take a moment to notice what is going on around you using your five senses. Take a few slow, deep breaths to help you to stay in the present.

Meditate

Meditation involves sitting quietly with your eyes closed and clearing your mind of thoughts. Meditation is a tool to relieve stress and help you focus only on the present. Instructions for meditating are provided in *13. Be Kind to Your Whole Self (pg. 77)*.

CHASE YOUR FEARS

Are you ever a little scared to try new things, meet new people or go to new places? Or maybe you're more scared of heights or dogs or bugs or getting up and speaking in front of a room full of people?

Fears can be like big monsters that leave us frozen in our tracks. We might not want to face the monsters because we don't think we can defeat them. They're strange and different from anything we've ever faced before, so we don't know whether we believe in ourselves enough to think we can defeat the monster. And if we lose, then we'll feel bad about ourselves and other people might make fun of us.

The truth is that fear isn't a monster at all. It's normal to be scared of trying new things, but those things are only as scary as our mind imagines them to be. And if you act bravely and chase your fears instead of letting them chase you away from trying new things, you just might find that they run away and disappear.

> **It's normal to be scared of trying new things, but those things are only as scary as our mind imagines them to be.**

Besides, you've probably defeated these monsters before and didn't even realize it. Have you ever been afraid to go to a new school but you went anyway? Or maybe there was a time when you felt scared to talk to kids you didn't know, but you said something anyway and ended up being friends? Those are times when you faced the fear monster with great success.

What if you had run away from those fears instead? What if you ran away from a lot of other fears too? If you were too scared to try things, you would miss out on a lot of good things and you might never grow up to do as much as you are really capable of doing. What if you could be a teacher who helps thousands of students learn, but you were too scared to get up in front of the class and speak, so you never tried? What if you could be so good at gymnastics that you could one day make it to the Olympic Games, but you felt too scared of heights to get up on the balance beam?

Overcoming your fears can help you learn a lot about yourself and it can introduce you to new and exciting people, places, and things. The more fears you chase away, the more confident you will become. Facing your fears may scare you, but not facing your fears means you may miss out on life and not become all that you could be.

What's the Worst that Could Happen?

Name something you are too scared to do right now, but that you really want to do. Now ask yourself, "What's the worst that could happen if I tried?" Is that worst thing really so bad?

Have a Conversation With Fear

Pick something that scares you and talk to it. Remind the fear that you are capable and self-confident. Below are some examples of what you might say if you were afraid of thunder. Come up with some similar examples for your own fear.

Be self-confident: "Thunder, you are just a loud noise. You can't hurt me!" "I've faced my fears before. I know I can handle this." "You can't bully me. I don't have to listen to you."

Be logical: "Thunder is not actually dangerous—it is just the sound of air quickly moving after being heated by lightning."

Set realistic expectations: "Everyone gets scared sometimes. There's nothing wrong with me." "My feelings of fear are only temporary. I know they will pass."

Remember How Brave You Are

Every time you face a fear, you build self-confidence. Sometimes we are so relieved after we face the monster that we forget to stop and take notice of what a big accomplishment it was. Think back. Name something you were afraid to do but you did anyway, and answer the following questions.

✳ What thoughts and feelings did you have before you faced the fear?

✳ What thought did you have that convinced you to face the fear even though you were scared?

✳ While you were standing face-to-face with your fear, how did you feel? What did you think when you realized things were going ok?

✳ What were the positive consequences of facing your fear? How did you feel?

Plan to conquer the fear you named in the *What's the Worst that Could Happen* exercise (on the previous page) just like you conquered this previous fear that you're remembering now.

✳ Are the thoughts and feelings you have with the new fear similar to the ones you experienced with your previous fear?

✳ If you successfully overcame those unhelpful thoughts and unpleasant feelings once before, doesn't that mean you are capable of doing it again?

✳ What thought did you have last time that enabled you to take action and face the fear? Try applying a similar thought to your current fear to motivate yourself to face it.

CUT YOUR PROBLEMS INTO PIECES

C ould you swallow an entire watermelon whole? Probably not. What if you cut the watermelon into smaller pieces and ate it bite by bite? That would make it easier, right? Sometimes you might face problems or tasks that seem as big as that watermelon. If you stuff that whole problem into your mouth without thinking, trying to solve it all in one big bite, you might find you've bitten off more than you can chew. That might make you spit the problem out and say, "There's no way I can handle a problem this big. I give up."

When watermelon-sized problems come your way, try cutting the problem into smaller bite-sized pieces instead. Taking charge of the problem and breaking it up into smaller steps that you can tackle one at a time will make you much more likely to succeed.

Let's say you have to clean your bedroom, and it is really messy. Really, really messy. There are clothes on the floor, your bed isn't made, your closet is overflowing, you can't close your dresser drawers, and you have shoved so much stuff under the bed that you can't even remember what's there anymore. That sounds like a watermelon-sized task. Let's break it down into smaller steps:

Step 1: Make the bed.

Step 2: Pick up the dirty clothes and put them in the dirty clothes hamper.

Step 3: Hang up clean clothes in your closet or fold them and put them in a drawer.

Step 4: Pull everything out from under the bed and either throw it away or put it where it belongs.

Step 5: Neatly re-fold the items in your drawers so that they all fit inside.

Now all you have to do is go through the list, one step at a time until all five are complete. Check off each step after you're done to keep track of how much you've accomplished. Before you know it, your room will be cleaner than you ever thought you could make it.

Slice Your Own Watermelon

Think of a problem or school assignment that seems too big for you to complete in one step. How could you break that problem down into smaller pieces that you know you can complete?

Slice It Again

What if the pieces you sliced are still too big? Don't worry—you can do one of two things. First, you can take a break while eating each piece. Second, you can just slice them again into smaller pieces. Let's look at step 3 from the room cleaning example in this section. You could hang and fold clothes for 15 minutes and then take a break for 10 minutes. You would repeat the 15 minutes of work and 10 minutes of break time until you completed step 3. Alternatively, you could split step 3 into two separate steps. Step 3a would be, "Hang up any clothes that belong on hangers and put them in the closet." Step 3b would be, "Fold any remaining clothes and put them in a dresser drawer." You could also take a break between the two steps.

Now you try: Make the steps you created in the first exercise a little easier to swallow by building in breaks or slicing steps into even smaller pieces.

Slice It, Portion It, and Refrigerate

What if you didn't have to finish eating your watermelon until two weeks from now? It's still important to plan ahead—otherwise you may end up having to eat the entire thing right before it's due. So, you would cut up the entire watermelon

The next time you get a long-term assignment, cut it into pieces and divide up the portions of work over the number of days you have until it's due.

into pieces and then divide each of the pieces evenly into fourteen bowls. You'd eat one portion, and then stick the other bowls in the refrigerator. For the next thirteen days, you would eat one portion of watermelon until the final day arrived. By eating a little bit every day, you make sure you won't ever get too full.

You can follow the same strategy for big assignments or projects that are due in the future. The next time you get this kind of assignment, cut it into pieces and divide up the portions of work over the number of days you have until it's due. You might want to make a calendar and mark which steps you have to complete each day. Then mark an "X" on the calendar when you complete each day's steps.

CONQUER PROBLEMATIC PROCRASTINATION

magine you are heading home from school knowing you have about 20 minutes of math homework and 15 minutes of English homework to do. You dread it. You can't stop thinking about how much you *don't* want to do it. So, when you get home, you play video games or go outside with your friends, and you put off doing that homework for as long as you possibly can. Has this ever happened to you? Putting off tasks that we could do now until a later time is called *procrastination*.

While there are lots of different reasons we put off doing certain things, our beliefs play an important role. Do you think that all activities should be relatively easy and stress-free? Do you think, "This task is way too unpleasant, and I can't stand unpleasant feelings"? This is called *discomfort intolerance*. Discomfort intolerance means that when you feel a certain level of anxiety or frustration about completing a task, you think to yourself, "I can't take it!"

The beliefs you have about yourself—your *self-esteem*—can also play a role in procrastination. If you don't see yourself as a person of worth who is smart and capable and who has a lot to be proud of, you may put off certain activities because you are afraid you will fail. For example, you may dread doing your homework if you think, "I never get grades as good as my classmates on these assignments. I'm useless in math and English."

Another reason you might put off doing homework or some other task is because it just isn't very interesting or fun. If math and English are two subjects that sometimes put you to sleep, you might think, "I can't bring myself to do this assignment. It's soooo boring!" So, given the choice between doing something boring and doing something fun—like playing video games or hanging out with your friends—you choose fun!

Putting off work until a later time doesn't always have negative consequences. In fact, sometimes you may have a logical reason for putting off doing a task. Let's say you have to write a report for school on the topic of endangered species. There's a great book available through your school's interlibrary loan system; however, it will take about one week for it to arrive, and your report is due in two weeks. You could use a couple of old magazines on your bookshelf, but you know the library book will provide you with more detailed information. After checking to make sure you will have plenty of time to work on the report next week after school, you decide to put off doing the report until the book arrives. In this case, you're not putting off the task because you're worried you'll fail or because you're afraid it's too hard and you can't take being frustrated, but because you know you that your report will be better if you wait a week until the book arrives.

In other cases, however, procrastination can become a problem. Do you procrastinate so much that you end up turning in a lot of late homework assignments, or not turning them in at all? Are your grades lower because of your procrastination? Do you put off doing your chores so often and for so long that they don't get done, and then you get punished? When you don't get things done because of your procrastination, do you develop unhelpful thoughts (like, "I can't do anything right," or "I'm no good,") and stressful emotions, (like anxiety or depression) that lead you to doubt yourself or to stop trying certain things? These are all signs of problematic procrastination.

Overcome Problematic Procrastination and Persevere

To persevere in life, it's important to accept that we all have to do *some* things that are difficult, boring, or otherwise unpleasant. Washing the dishes or cleaning up your room may not always be enjoyable, but these are things that are necessary to keep our living environment clean. That's important to our lifelong health. Similarly, homework may be a chore, but it serves an important purpose in the long run. Not only does homework help to reinforce new information and skills, but doing your homework regularly teaches you important life skills like problem-solving, critical thinking, time management, and self-discipline. Keeping the long-term benefit of a task in

Making yourself do the things that are unpleasant to you can be an effective way to overcome problematic procrastination.

mind may remind you why learning to tolerate a short-term discomfort is so important. Without patience and perseverance, you may not reach where you want to go.

It may seem hard to believe, but making yourself do the things that are unpleasant to you can be an effective way to overcome problematic procrastination. That's because of the overwhelmingly positive feeling you get from completing the task. You prove to yourself that you can do it and that gives you the confidence to know you could do it again.

So how do you "just do it"? To make it through an unpleasant task, there are several things you can try.

Challenge unhelpful beliefs. Unhelpful beliefs about yourself or about a task are often at the root of problematic procrastination. So, to change your behavior, challenge these beliefs. Do you have a low tolerance for discomfort? Try telling yourself, "I don't like doing this, but I can handle it."

Are you impatient? Do you expect everything to be pretty easy and avoid things when they're not? Remind yourself, "I'd prefer if I didn't have to work hard at this, but I know I can't get everything I want instantly." (And be sure to check out *14. Practice Being Patient [pg. 81]* for more tips on learning patience and overcoming the instant gratification itch.)

If your inner voice is saying negative things about you— like that you're not smart enough or that you'll never be as good as any of your friends—then try to raise your self-esteem by hushing these negative voices. *1. Have a Positive Attitude (pg. 9)* can help you recognize your strengths and learn how to develop a more positive attitude toward yourself.

Break up the task. Learning to see tasks as several small pieces instead of as one big whole can make them seem more doable. For example, you could think of your math homework as a big set of 20 problems, or you could think of it as 4 smaller sets of

> **When an unhelpful thought enters your mind or you notice yourself feeling tense, breathe deeply, allow the thought to pass through, repeat a positive phrase in your mind, and then re-focus on the work at hand.**

only 5 problems each. Which seems easier to complete? Set a goal to finish five problems in one sitting. Then, after a short break, complete another five problems. Then do two more sessions of five problems each until the set of twenty is complete. Before you know it, you've finished!

Take breaks. It's important not to let yourself get too frustrated, anxious, or tense because those emotions can make it hard to get yourself calm and focused. One way to keep unhelpful thoughts and difficult emotions in check is to schedule breaks in advance. If you know you're about to do something that frustrates you, plan to work for five minutes and then take a break for five minutes. Continue working and taking breaks every five minutes until the task is complete. If you still notice the early signs of frustration—tension in your head, face, neck, and shoulders; a knot in your stomach; feeling antsy; squirming in your chair; and having a hard time staying focused— allow yourself to take a short break, even if it's before you had planned on it. Adjust your plan as often as you need until you find the right balance between work and breaks.

Your goal during breaks is to try to relax and prepare yourself to go back to the task. During the break, practice breathing deeply and trying to clear your mind. It may also help you to repeat a positive slogan like, "I don't like this, but I can handle it."

Breathe. Controlling your breathing can help you control your anxiety and frustration. Sometimes, when we get tense, we hold our breath or only breathe very lightly. Pay attention to your breathing as you work, and make a point of breathing slowly and deeply. To do this, breathe from your belly. As you inhale, let your stomach move out. As you exhale, your stomach should contract inward.

Is Procrastination a Problem for You?

Can you think of a time when putting off a task resulted in a negative consequence for you? Some examples of negative consequences include punishment, a bad grade or incomplete assignment, or difficult emotions (experiencing worry, doubt, or insecurity about your abilities). What led you to put off this task? Is it boring? Does it make you frustrated or anxious? Work with a parent, teacher, or school counselor to help yourself identify why you put off a task and write them down on a piece of paper.

Make a Plan to Overcome Problematic Procrastination

On the piece of paper containing the list of unhelpful thoughts that you just created, write down statements that challenge each thought. For example, if you thought you wouldn't succeed in completing the task, you could write, "I've been able to finish pretty much everything I've tried in the past, so I believe I can successfully finish this, too."

Next, decide whether you will complete the task in one sitting, or whether you will break it up into smaller parts and take breaks in between. Be specific about your goals and what you hope to accomplish during each stage, and decide how long your breaks will be. Remember to leave your frustration or unhelpful thoughts behind when you come back to the task after a break.

Try to concentrate only on the task at hand while you're working. When an unhelpful thought enters your mind or you notice yourself feeling tense, breathe deeply, allow the thought to pass through, repeat a positive phrase in your mind, and then re-focus on the work at hand. When you're finished, make note of how you feel. Modify the plan as needed.

On the Count of 3 ... Go Do It!

For tough tasks, you may find it helpful to plan things out or take breaks like you did in the first exercises. But for tasks you know you can do that you simply don't like, it's sometimes better to stop thinking about it and force yourself to get up and get moving. Instead of putting off taking out the garbage or picking up your dirty clothes and spending the rest of the evening thinking about how much you don't want to do it, stop what you're doing and just go do it.

Right now, decide on a task that you can complete. When you're finished, take a moment to pay attention to what you're feeling. How does it feel to know that you've finished this task and you don't have to worry about it anymore?

Put Things in Perspective

Sometimes it helps to remind ourselves that it's important to persevere through a bit of short-term frustration so that we can achieve our long-term goals. Make a list of things that frustrate you or that you find yourself putting off because you don't enjoy them. Beside each task, write down the long-term benefit to you of doing that task. That long-term benefit could be something directly positive (for example, math homework teaches you problem-solving skills that you can apply to your life or job) or it could be something that prevents a negative (for example, doing dishes keeps me from getting sick). Below is an example:

Task	Long-Term Advantage
Reading a book	Reading is an important skill I will need in everyday life. As I grow up, I will need to be able to read to get a good job and to take care of myself. Reading stories can also show me how to use my imagination and be creative.

EXPAND
YOUR WORLD

Have you ever used your imagination to dream about another universe or far-off lands? Did those places seem really different from the world in which you live? Do you think it would be fun to visit places that are really different from your own, and that have different types of food, people, and animals?

Well, you don't have to travel to another planet or watch a science-fiction movie to experience someplace new and interesting. There are lots of places right here on earth. The planet you live on is made up of many pieces that all connect and interlock with one another. The pieces represent people and cultures from every country and continent across the globe. Every piece of the puzzle is equally important. As a citizen of the world, you have your very own piece of the puzzle, and that means you have an important role, too.

Environmental and Social Responsibility

All global citizens have a responsibility to take care of the earth
and help each other. This is called environmental and social
responsibility. You have the power to help protect wildlife;
keep oceans, lakes and rivers clean; plant trees; and help to
preserve parks and rainforests. You can also help people
anywhere on earth who may be suffering because of poverty,
war, or other problems. Your world will expand whenever you
take time to appreciate the different cultural traditions of your
neighbors around the world.

Because the pieces of the world puzzle are all connected,
every little thing you do affects the puzzle pieces around you.
Then those pieces affect pieces around them, and the effect
keeps spreading and spreading until every piece in the whole
world is touched. For example, if you choose to pick up a piece
of litter from the ground, you might save the life of animals
that could have eaten that trash and become sick. Because
those animals are still alive, they can enrich their natural
habitat. Then that will allow more animals to thrive and grow.
So you have helped improve wildlife and nature, all by picking
up one little piece of trash.

Environmental and social responsibility teaches you compassion. When you expand your world, you take the focus off
of yourself and become aware of others. As you encounter
new cultures, you may at first think you don't have much in

> **Because the pieces of the world puzzle are
> all connected, every little thing you do affects
> the puzzle pieces around you.**

common with them. But if you look more closely and think about how people in these other cultures think and feel and behave, you'll find that you have a lot more in common than you think. Exploring other cultures helps you to develop empathy and a desire to act with kindness. And when you do kind things for others, you not only help them, but you boost your self-esteem. By taking pride in the things you do to protect nature or help kids in other countries, you learn the value of hard work and caring. Empathy, compassion, hard work, pride, and responsibility can make you happier, healthier, more socially confident, and more successful in reaching your own personal goals.

Connect With Your Neighbors Across the Country

Once a month, pick a state in the United States. With the help of a teacher or parent, do some research to learn about the environmental and social issues of that state. Environmental issues would include things relating to the state's wildlife and habitat, and social issues include things like poverty, food and water problems, and homelessness. Find at least one thing you can identify with that makes you experience compassion or empathy. What could you do as an act of kindness? Some examples include sending food donations to a shelter in the state you're researching, or contributing a small donation to a state wildlife charity. Can you think of any others?

Connect With Your Neighbors Across the Globe

Once a month, pick a country anywhere in the world outside of the United States (maybe a country or continent you would like to travel to one day). With the help of a parent or teacher, do some research using books or the computer. Find out about that country's customs, language, music, food, habitat, and animals, as well as any environmental and social issues. List some things about that culture that are different, and at least one thing you identified with that was similar to something you've experienced. Find one thing that makes you have empathy and compassion, and name something kind you could do in response to any difficulties you found the country or its citizens have.

Be Responsible in Your Neighborhood

There are plenty of opportunities in your neighborhood to be environmentally and socially responsible. Name three things you can do and decide when you will do them. For example, you could pledge to visit a soup kitchen to feed the homeless once a month and to keep your surroundings clean and the earth and animals healthy by picking up litter every day.

SPEAK FOR YOURSELF

Everyone has an inner voice. It's that voice that won't stop bugging us whenever we're thinking about doing something we know we're not supposed to. It's the one that says, "You know it's not nice to make fun of someone," or, "You know better than to cheat." Sometimes you might think that voice is trying to spoil your fun, but it's really just trying to help you make the best choices you can—choices that will make you feel good about yourself.

That inner voice can have an especially hard time competing with the voices of your friends or schoolmates. Other people can put a lot of pressure on you to join in with them to do things that you know in your gut are not very nice. You might be tempted to go along with those things because you want other kids to like you. When you do something because you're worried your classmates and friends will make fun of you if you don't, then you've given in to *peer pressure*. Other times, you may go along with something because you don't

Socially confident kids develop good social skills—they can communicate well with others and they have good manners.

have as much confidence as you need to speak for yourself. Or you may be threatened by someone else. In that case, you are being *bullied*.

Whether you're facing bullying or peer pressure, you can learn to speak for yourself by improving your *social confidence*. Social confidence is believing in your ability to interact with your peers effectively. Socially confident kids develop good social skills—they can communicate well with others and they have good manners. Social skills and social confidence are something you learn over time through lots of practice. Here are some other tips to help get you started on becoming confident enough to speak for yourself.

Get confident. Bullies are more likely to pick on kids they think won't stand up for themselves. The more self-confident you are, the less likely you are to be bullied or pressured into doing something you don't want to do. Build your self-confidence over time by practicing your social skills and getting involved in activities you like and you're good at, such as martial arts or team sports. It's just as important to look self-confident as it is to feel your self-confidence. Carry your shoulders back and your head up. Don't hunch over or stare at the floor, because that gives the impression that you are unsure of yourself. Look people in the eye when they speak to you, as that's also a sign of self-confidence.

Watch and listen. A great way to learn how to handle social situations is to watch what other people do. Can you identify the kids in your class who are socially confident? How can you tell? What is different about their posture or the way they talk? Listening is also very important, for two reasons. First, listening to what another person is saying makes that person understand that he is liked, so it can help you make friends. Second, listening to what people say and how they say it can help you learn what works well and what doesn't work well in social situations.

Be assertive. Being assertive means that you confidently say what you think and feel in a way that doesn't attack others or put them down. For example, an assertive person might say, "I'm upset that you haven't returned my book yet because I need it for class today. I'd like for you to give it back to me."

Some people confuse assertiveness with aggression. Aggression is a hostile or threatening way of communicating. Aggression is what bullies use to get others to do what they want. A bully might say, "Give me my book or I'm going to punch you."

On the other extreme, there's passiveness or submissiveness. People who are passive do not stand up for themselves. They are unlikely to say what they think or feel at all. A passive person might be too uncertain of himself to even ask for the book back even though he really needs it. Assertiveness is the middle ground, and it's the type of communication that socially skilled people use.

Practice your communication skills. When you are trying to stick up for yourself or others, what you say and how you say it can make all the difference. Avoid blaming, criticizing, yelling, or threatening. Instead, speak calmly and assertively. Assertive statements often come in the form, "I am [fill in the blank] because [fill in the blank], and I would like it if you would [fill in the blank]." For example, "I am frustrated because you're not participating in this group assignment, and I would like it if you would please help out with the project." You can also try a *win-win statement*. That means you say assertively what you are feeling (a win for you) and you convince the other person that playing by the rules is a win for them too. For example, let's say you catch someone cheating while you're playing a game. You might say, "It's just a game. It's not that important who wins. It's more fun for everyone when we all play fairly." You spoke up because you didn't approve of the cheating, and—without criticizing the person—you tried to get him to see that everyone could win if he would stop cheating.

Don't be afraid to leave. You may find yourself in social situations that you just don't want to be in. You don't always have to speak up. Sometimes it's best just to leave. If you are unsafe or are around kids that you know are bullies, just walk away. If they speak to you, just pretend you don't hear them and keep walking. And if you are afraid someone else there could get hurt, tell an adult.

Get a Feel for Assertiveness

Learning how to be assertive will build the confidence that will help you stick up for yourself when you need to. Below are examples of social situations you might find yourself in. Write down the aggressive, passive, and assertive ways to handle the situation. Use the first example as a guide.

Situation: John wants to skip class and is trying to convince others to do the same. You don't want to go.

Aggressive: "If you don't stop asking me, I'm going to beat you up."

Passive: "I don't really want to skip class, but I won't tell on you if you do."

Assertive: "I don't agree with what you're doing. I'm not going to skip class."

Situation: You watch Simone try to convince Andrea to steal the teacher's pen from her desk when her back is turned. Andrea really doesn't want to do it, but she's afraid to say "no." What would you say to Simone?

Aggressive:

Passive:

Assertive:

Situation: You and your friend Mark want to play soccer. Several other kids are already playing a game. You walk up to them and ask if you can join.

Aggressive:

Passive:

Assertive:

Practice Speaking for Yourself

The more prepared you are for social situations, the more confident you will be about your ability to handle them. Choose one of the following situations and act it out with a friend, sibling, parent, or teacher. If possible, have an adult watch you and give you feedback on your performance. Try to use the assertive or win-win communication styles explained in this section.

Situation: Molly is using the library computer. Derrick walks over and grabs the mouse and forces her to get out of her chair so he can take her spot. What should Molly do?

Situation: Samantha, Eric, and several other kids are playing a game. Samantha sees that Eric cheated. What should Samantha do?

Find a Good Model

You can learn a lot from watching how others handle difficult social situations. Do a little research and find an example of a character in a movie, television show, book, or play who sticks up for what he or she believes in. Answer the following questions:

1. Describe the situation. How did the character end up there? Was he or she convinced to be there by others, or did he or she go willingly?

2. When did the character stick up for him- or herself? Do you think things would have been different if he or she had said something earlier or not gone at all?

3. Write down the words the character said. Was the character assertive?

4. What were the consequences of the character sticking up for him- or herself? Were the consequences all positive? Did the character lose friends or get in trouble? Is losing friends because of sticking up for yourself necessarily a negative consequence, or is there another way to look at it?

FORGIVE TO FEEL BETTER

When people do or say things that hurt you, what do you do? Do you say or do something mean back to them? Do you give them the silent treatment? Do you hold a grudge against them?

Sometimes, even if people apologize, it can be hard to let go of how angry and upset we are. We might think that refusing to forgive someone is a way to punish them for hurting us. But when you hold a grudge, you are also holding all of those related emotions inside of you. When you carry those emotions around with you for a long time, they can start to eat you up inside. Your stomach might start hurting, you might get a headache, and your body might feel tense all over. You think you're punishing the other person, but really you are just punishing yourself. In fact, people who are better at forgiving are less likely to be really anxious, depressed, or hostile and are more likely to feel physically healthier.

Forgiving people is a way for you to get rid of those hurtful emotions inside of yourself and get on with your life. Sometimes people don't want to forgive because they misunderstand what it means.

When you forgive someone, it does NOT mean

* that it was ok for that person to hurt you

* that you will just forget what happened

* that you are weak

When you forgive someone, it DOES mean

* that you understand that everyone makes bad choices and mistakes sometimes

* that you don't want to stay angry and hurt over what happened because that isn't healthy for you

* that you have decided to let go of what happened so that you can feel better and be happy

It can take a long time to truly get over certain things, and just because you've forgiven someone doesn't mean you have to be best friends with them again unless you think that it's right for you. Forgiveness is simply a way for you to get on with your life and leave the hurtful emotions behind you.

Self-Forgiveness

Sometimes, the person we are angry with isn't someone else—it's ourselves. Maybe you're disappointed with how you did on a test or you're upset because you said something that caused your mom hurt feelings. If you are having a hard time forgiving yourself, it may be because you're expecting too

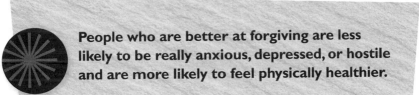

People who are better at forgiving are less likely to be really anxious, depressed, or hostile and are more likely to feel physically healthier.

much. Do you think it's realistic to expect that you will never make mistakes on tests? Is it likely that you'll never get really mad and say something that you didn't really mean? Unless we learn to forgive ourselves for our mistakes, we will end up beating ourselves up. Just like you can make yourself physically ill from holding a grudge against someone else, you can do the same when you hold a grudge against yourself. Negative thoughts and emotions can also hurt your self-esteem. Taking steps to forgive ourselves is just as important as taking steps to forgive others.

The Process of Forgiving

Most people can't simply say or think, "I forgive you," and move on. For the majority of us, forgiveness is a journey. If we take small steps toward forgiveness each day, we will eventually get there. Here are a few ways to work toward letting go of your grudge.

Switch shoes. Later in this book, in section *16. Switch Shoes (pg. 93),* you will learn more about how helpful it can be to put yourself in another person's shoes. By trying to understand that person's thoughts, feelings, and personal experiences, you may develop compassion. You may know what it feels like to go through some of their difficulties, so you may develop empathy for them.

Visualize forgiveness. Close your eyes and create a mental picture of yourself sitting down and talking to the person you are angry with. Keep calm by breathing slowly and deeply. Imagine yourself saying exactly how you feel and understand why it's so important to forgive this person. Imagine that person responding exactly as you wish they would.

Monitor your thoughts and expectations. Your inner voice may want to remind you how angry you are. That's normal, but it's not useful when you're trying to forgive. Respond by saying, "I am angry, but I'm determined to work hard to forgive so I can be peaceful again."

Your inner voice may also sound frustrated, saying things like, "Why can't I forgive yet?" Respond by reminding your inner voice to keep realistic expectations: "Forgiveness takes time. I just have to practice patience and keep trying."

Express Your Feelings

A) **Role-play by yourself.** For this exercise, you will need two chairs. Place the chairs several feet apart, facing each other. You will sit in one chair. The other chair will remain empty. Pretend the person you are angry with is sitting in that chair. Tell that person how you feel as a result of what he or she did.

B) **Draw two pictures.** In the first picture, portray the argument or situation that made you angry. In the second picture, portray what it would look like for you to forgive.

C) Write a letter. You will not mail this letter or show it to anyone. It is for you to express the personal thoughts and emotions you wish the other person could know and understand. You could also keep a daily journal where you write down your feelings, or write daily letters.

D) Role-play. Work with your mom, dad, sibling, teacher, or counselor to role-play forgiveness. In the first role-play, play yourself as you express your emotions and try to forgive. In the second role-play, take on the role of the person who upset you. Portray how you would like for that person to respond.

Find Common Ground

Think of a situation in which you're having a hard time forgiving someone. Switch shoes and consider what it is like to be the person you are angry with. Find at least one emotion or thought you share in common—maybe you are both frustrated by math homework, maybe you both have been teased at school, or maybe you both get bored and have a hard time sitting still in class. Use that commonality to help yourself develop empathy and compassion for the other person.

Forgive Yourself

A) Switch shoes. Think of a situation where you're having a hard time forgiving yourself. Pretend you are one of your friends and you are looking at the situation from his or her perspective. As your friend, you try to understand what thoughts, emotions, and situations led to your behavior so that you can develop compassion. What would your friend say to show empathy and kindness toward you? If your friend can forgive you, can you see things from his perspective and forgive yourself too?

B) List expectations. Take out a sheet of paper and draw a line down the center from top to bottom. On the left-hand side, write "things I expect from myself." Make a list of your expectations. For example, "I expect myself never to hurt other people," or, "I expect myself always to get a B+ or better on tests." For each one, decide whether it is realistic or not realistic. If it is realistic, write "R" in the right-hand column. If it is not realistic, use the right-hand column to rephrase the expectation so that it becomes realistic. For example, "I will try not to hurt people, but everyone makes mistakes so I may hurt someone sometime." Discuss these statements with your parents, teacher, or counselor.

C) Write a letter to yourself. In the letter, express why you are disappointed or angry, but also show yourself compassion and explain why it's important to forgive you.

BE KIND TO
YOUR WHOLE SELF

Pretend once again that you are an astronaut trying
to achieve your mission to keep yourself feeling good.
    If Mission Control (your mind) keeps sending negative
messages over and over again—saying things like, "This
mission is hopeless," or, "I don't believe you can accomplish
the goal,"—you may not only start to be hurt or sad, but you
may become physically ill. You may feel sick to your stomach
and or have aches and pains in your body. The reverse is also
true. If you stop eating your astronaut meals and don't do your
morning exercise and stretching, your body will not be fit or
healthy. As your body weakens, it sends signals to Mission
Control that you are not strong and well. Then, your thoughts
about yourself become more negative.
    Your mind and your body make up your whole self. They
work in unison, so what one feels, so does the other. When
you smile, your body sends a signal to your brain that you are
happy. When you are happy, you think positive thoughts. So
your brain, emotions, and physical body work in harmony.

What you think affects how you feel and act, and how you behave affects what you think and feel. So, to feel good, it's important to be kind to your whole self.

Eat well. To feel good, it's best to avoid eating too many sugary or processed foods. Processed foods are those that have preservatives, chemicals, or sweeteners added to them to make them taste better or help them last longer. Packaged cookies, crackers, and cakes that you find in the grocery aisle are some common examples. Processed foods and sugar can affect your mood in unhealthy ways. They can also cause you to gain weight and you can develop other health problems if you eat too many of them. If you can, try to eat fresh fruits and vegetables and lean proteins like chicken, fish, and beans to keep your body healthy and full of energy.

Get enough sleep. Getting between 9 and 11 hours of sleep every night is important for kids your age. If you don't get enough sleep, your brain doesn't work as well as when you do get that sleep. You have a harder time learning new things or remembering things. Sleep deprivation can also affect your emotions and make you grouchy and impatient. Your body feels more tired, and it's harder to get moving. Going to bed at the same time every night can help you get in the habit of getting a full night's sleep.

Have good hygiene. Hygiene means cleanliness. Keeping your body clean can prevent you from catching colds and viruses. Brushing your teeth and flossing at least twice a day and taking baths or showers several times a week will keep you clean. One

Pick one healthy thing to do each day for a week.

of the most important things you can do to prevent yourself from getting sick is to wash your hands. Washing your hands every time before you eat and after you use the bathroom can keep you from catching and spreading infections.

Laugh a lot. Did you know that laughing can improve your health? Laughing causes certain chemicals to start flowing through your bloodstream. As those chemicals move through your body, they ease stress and make you happy. They can even relieve physical pain. Laughing with other people—like when you're playing a game, watching a movie, or telling stories or jokes—is a great way to keep the laughter going and to grow close and connected to others.

Relieve stress. There are lots of different ways to relieve stress. It is a good idea to try different activities and see which one works best for you. Some helpful stress relievers include exercise, deep breathing, blowing bubbles, jumping rope, playing games, putting a puzzle together, listening to music, or engaging in visualization or meditation. Physical touch—like getting and giving hugs or massages—can also help ease tension. Next time you're stressed out, try hugging your mom or getting her to rub your shoulders.

Meditate

Find a quiet spot at home where you won't be interrupted. Sit on the floor cross-legged. Put a pillow underneath you if it's more comfortable. Lay your hands in your lap, or rest your wrists on your knees with your hands face-up. Close your eyes. Notice your breath as you inhale and exhale slowly. Clear your mind of thoughts. If thoughts pop into your head—like, "I really want to open my eyes," or, "I'm worried about the test tomorrow,"— just let them pass through and try to re-focus yourself on meditating.

Prove to Yourself How Good Healthy Feels

We don't always pay attention to how our choices make us feel. Try to become more aware by linking what you do with what you feel. Pick one healthy thing to do daily for a week. You could pledge to eat vegetables twice a day (maybe once at lunch and again at dinner); to do something active (like walk, run, or play sports) once a day after school; to set a limit on video game or TV time and replace that with an outdoor activity; or to give yourself a strict bedtime to make sure you get enough sleep. Each time you do that healthy thing, write down in a journal how you feel afterward. Do you have more energy? Do you sleep better? Look back at your journal entries to see the positive effects of your new healthy behaviors.

Experiment With Stress Relief

Try out different stress relievers to help you discover what works best for you. Below is a short list of things people sometimes do to relieve stress and clear their minds:

✳ Singing or listening to music
✳ Deep breathing
✳ Meditation
✳ Physical exercise like skateboarding, soccer, or tennis
✳ Reading a book

Add some more ideas to the list and give them each a try. Before you do that healthy thing, write down how you feel. Then, after you do it, describe how your body feels. Do you feel more relaxed? Is your mind less cloudy?

PRACTICE BEING PATIENT

Have you ever tried to walk across a field of high grass? The first time you walk across it, you have to lift your feet high, and each step takes a lot of effort. But, if you go back the next day and try to walk across it again, you might be able to find the path you took the day before where the grass has been flattened, making it easier for you to walk. If you went back each day and walked that same path, the grass would get flatter and flatter, and the walk would get easier and easier.

That's exactly what happens in your brain when you practice something every day. The first time you play an instrument or practice your handwriting, it's really hard because your brain has never done it before. You have to blaze a new trail in your mind. Every note and every movement of the pencil takes a lot of effort while you try to figure it out. But each time you practice, your brain remembers where you left off the last time, and it gets a little bit easier until eventually you can play or write without even thinking about it.

The same is true of practicing patience. At first, waiting for anything is hard. Waiting in line at the store, waiting for dinner to be ready, or waiting for your turn to play a game can take a lot of effort. But the more you practice patience, the easier it gets.

The Instant Gratification Itch

Your mom just got back from the grocery store. She bought a bag of your favorite chocolate candy treats. The moment you see her take them out of the shopping bag, you ask her if you can have some. She tells you that if you wait until she is finished unloading the groceries from the car, she will give you two treats. As soon as she heads back out to the car, you have a sudden urge to rip open the bag. It's so hard to resist. It's like an itch you can't scratch and it's driving you crazy. You can't wait until she's done unloading the groceries. You scratch the itch, helping yourself to a big handful of the candy. Then you run out of the kitchen, only to get in trouble once your mom finds out.

That urge or uncomfortable itch, like the urge to have the candy now instead of later, is for *instant gratification*. That means when you see or do something, you want to reap the rewards from it immediately. You don't have the patience to wait for long or to make a lot of effort—you just want the positive outcome *now*. People who have a hard time resisting scratching the instant gratification itch are impatient. They

People who have a hard time resisting scratching the instant gratification itch are impatient.

don't want to save their allowance money for several months in order to pay for a video game. They want their parents to buy it now. They don't want to spend weeks reading a long book. They want someone to just tell them what happens.

How to Keep Yourself From Scratching

So, how do you keep yourself from cutting in line or eating dessert first and spoiling your dinner? First, distract yourself by doing something else. When you're waiting in line to get on an amusement park ride, you could sing a song quietly to yourself or in your head or you could create a game—like counting the number of people you see wearing hats. Second, talk back to your inner voice. When it's saying, "I can't wait," tell it, "I'm a little antsy, but I've experienced this before and I know I can handle it." Look at all the other people in line to remind yourself that everyone has to wait sometimes. Third, help soothe the uncomfortable tension of impatience by breathing in and out, slowly and deeply. If you're fidgeting or tapping your foot, try to gradually slow down the pace of the tapping. Slow down your body like you're slowing down your breath. Ask yourself, "What's the rush?"

Play the Waiting Game

Whenever you're having a hard time being patient, pass the time by playing a game. If you're in a place where there are signs, flyers, or billboards, pick a word from the sign and try to rearrange its letters to make another word. Or, pick a color and search for everything around you that is that color. You could also write a poem or compose a song in your head. Can you think of any other games you could play to pass the time?

Don't Scratch the Itch

When you feel impatience building inside you and you want to give up, rush through something, or take a bite out of that pie, don't! Forcing yourself to delay gratification (to put off getting what you want) is a great way to learn patience.

A) **Wait.** Every day, force yourself to wait for something you want. For example, if you normally play video games the second you come home from school, force yourself to wait one hour every day before you play.

B) **Set a long-term goal.** If you really want to challenge yourself, make this long-term goal something that requires you to put in effort every day. For example, set a goal to see a new movie in one week. The only way you get to see the movie is if you complete a set of chores each day. You could also plan to get dinner from your favorite restaurant in one week if you complete your homework every day right after school. Work with your parents to help you carry out these plans.

Blaze a Trail in Your Brain

Rehearsing something over and over again will clear a path in your mind and make it easier to get to the reward. Setting up a routine practice schedule will help you build patience. Pick a task that you sometimes find yourself getting impatient with. It could be practicing a musical instrument, reading, spelling, doing math homework, or playing a sport. Commit to doing that task 15 minutes each day for 1 week.

CONTROL WHAT YOU CAN

Have you ever been really excited to go swimming, but then a big storm with lots of lightning and thunder rolled in and you couldn't go? Or maybe you were supposed to take a weekend trip to an amusement park with your family, but then your brother got sick so you had to put it off. Or maybe someone you thought was your friend didn't invite you to her birthday party. Some things that happen in life are beyond our control. There's nothing you could have done to stop the thunderstorm, keep your brother from getting sick, or make your friend give you an invitation. So, you can't control Mother Nature or illness or what other people say or do. But you can control one very important thing: you. You can control what you think, feel, and do.

> **You can't control Mother Nature or illness or what other people say or do.**

Your Personal Power

The one thing you are in control of is *you*. You decide how you think, feel, and act. It's not always easy to think, feel, and act in ways that make us feel good—it takes a lot of personal awareness and hard work. But if you put in the effort, you will develop self-confidence and become more and more capable of handling difficult situations.

Exercise self-control. Unfortunately, you can't control what other people do. But, by exercising self-control, you can keep yourself safe, out of trouble, and feeling good. Self-control means being able to think before you act. It means that you manage your emotions and actions in effective ways during stressful situations. For example, imagine you are at the park, playing kickball with some friends. Another kid comes up and yells at you to give him the ball. He then pushes you hard and grabs the ball away from you. You are very angry and instinctively want to push him back. But, you don't. You think about the consequences before you act. If you push him, he'll probably push back. Then, you'll probably get into a fight and you'll both get hurt or get in trouble. So, you decide to walk away. You took charge of the situation by controlling what you could—your own response.

Avoid blaming. You can't control a classmate's decision to tease you, but you can control how you respond to it. If you respond by thinking negative thoughts about yourself and avoiding school and your friends, you may then be tempted to blame your classmate for how you're feeling. Similarly, when really difficult things happen—like someone dies or there's a car accident or fire—it is human instinct to want to blame someone or something for it. You want to understand why it happened, so saying it's your friend's fault or your mom or dad's fault is one way of trying to make sense of it. But blaming means you're not taking personal responsibility for what's within your personal power to do. And it's within your personal power to bounce back and not let those types of things steer you away from your goals. That doesn't mean that you aren't sad or upset. It's normal to have those emotions. It just means you know that in order to feel good, you have to work hard to understand those emotions and persevere.

Take responsibility for the consequences of your actions. Accepting control over your actions also means taking responsibility for mistakes. Mistakes are normal. Everyone makes them. Sometimes you may say things you wish you hadn't. Or, even though you meant well, maybe something you did ended up upsetting someone. For example, maybe you took your older brother to play tennis with you, but when you got home, you found out your younger sister was upset because you didn't take her along, too. At that point you realize that you didn't consider taking her and you wish you would have. Just like it's not helpful to blame others, it's also not helpful to blame yourself. Instead, take responsibility for your actions by admitting your mistake. In this example, you could apologize to your sister, or take other action to make things better (for example, you could take your younger sister to play tennis with you the next day).

The Limits of Your Control and Personal Responsibility

Learning what you can and cannot control is tough. There are two things to understand. First, although you may think you're responsible, certain problems simply aren't your fault. Second, it's not within your personal power to fix every problem.

Imagine a loved one is sick. You think you are responsible for it because, once when you were really mad, you thought something mean in your head. You believe that this person is now getting punished because of your mean wish. But angry thoughts in our heads do not make bad things happen to other people or to you. Unfortunately, sometimes people just get sick, have accidents, or suffer other misfortunes. These types of things are not your fault.

Now, imagine your parents are getting divorced. Again, you think you're responsible. You think that you misbehaved too much or didn't finish your chores like you were supposed to and that's what caused your parents to split up. But what happens in your parents' relationship is beyond your personal control. You could get perfect grades, do all your chores, and never get in trouble, but that wouldn't bring your parents back together. What adults say and do is beyond your control, and you are not to blame for their decisions.

What to Do When Things Aren't in Your Control

When something happens that's beyond your control, there are two things you can do. First, instead of worrying about it, focus your thoughts on the things in your life you can control, like reaching your goals in school or sports. Second, find ways to reduce unhelpful thoughts and emotions related to the thing you can't control.

For example, let's consider the example of having a sick loved one. Although you can't fix the illness, you can show sympathy by doing something kind. You could make a drawing or card, bake some cookies, pick flowers, or write a nice letter to the person. Focus on providing comfort to the person, rather than trying to fix his or her illness. Repeat to yourself, "It's not my fault this person is sick and I can't fix it, but I can show them I care by being kind."

Coping with something like your parents getting divorced isn't easy, so you have to work at it every day. First, combat your unhelpful thoughts. Your inner voice may keep telling you it's your fault, so respond back by repeating, "I'm sad my parents are getting divorced, but I know it isn't because of me. It's not my responsibility or within my power to control adult relationships." Second, talk with your parents, teacher, or counselor about how you're feeling. They can help reassure you that things will be ok.

17. Spring Back (pg. 101) has more strategies to help you learn how to spring back from tough situations. Laughing with others and keeping a positive, optimistic outlook, exercising, breathing deeply, and engaging in creative visualization are all great ways to keep you on track.

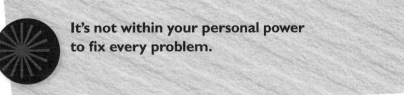

It's not within your personal power to fix every problem.

Understand the Limits of Your Control

It's important not to blame yourself or take responsibility for fixing problems that are beyond your control. Decide whether each of the following events is in your control or out of your control:

✻ Your mom and dad having an argument
✻ Your favorite teacher retiring
✻ Getting an "incomplete" on your homework assignment
✻ Calling a classmate a mean name
✻ Your grandfather going to the hospital
✻ Moving to another house or town
✻ Eating a lot of cake and feeling sick to your stomach

Can you think of any other situations that are beyond your control?

Make Your Life a No-Blame Zone

When someone else says or does something that upsets us and we struggle to bounce back, we may be tempted to blame them. But blaming or bad-mouthing others just takes away your personal power. From this point forward, make a vow not to blame anyone or anything for your problems. Tell your parents and teachers about your pledge so they can help make sure you're sticking to it.

To get you started on the right track, think of a time you blamed someone for something. What could you have done to control your response to the situation so that you didn't blame anyone?

Take Control of Your Mistakes

Admitting you made a mistake shows that you are confident
in yourself and that you have compassion for other people.
The next time you make a mistake, commit to apologizing
or taking steps to make the problem less of a big deal. Tell a
parent, teacher, or counselor that you made a mistake and ask
for their help in coming up with a plan to take responsibility
for it.

SWITCH SHOES

Who is your favorite movie or television actor? What character did he or she play that you really liked? When actors play a role, they put themselves in the character's shoes. To really understand what it's like to be the character, they spend time studying his or her background: what dreams and goals the character has, what the character thinks and believes about him- or herself and the world, and what family or cultural factors have influenced the character. Actors also look for something about the character they can personally relate to or find a similarity between them. By doing this, actors feel closer to the characters they play. They can identify with some part of the character. They care about the character.

In real life, we can use the same strategy to understand others. When we tune in to what other people feel, think, and believe, we are better able to understand why they act in certain ways or say the things they do. And the better we understand them, the more we care. This leads us to have sympathy and empathy. Sympathy is having care and concern for someone else's misfortunes. When we say we feel sorry for someone, we usually mean we are sympathetic. Empathy means that you can really identify with another person's troubles because you have experienced something similar. When you are empathetic, you will often experience some of the same emotions and thoughts as the other person. Sympathy and empathy develop as you become aware of how much we all have in common. Although we may have different attitudes and beliefs, we're all still human and struggle with many of the same things. If, like an actor, you look for these commonalities in others, you will develop compassion and kindness.

If someone else lived your life for a day and walked in your shoes, what would he or she find out about you? Are you grumpy in the mornings because you don't get enough sleep? Do you have a brother or sister who picks on you a lot? Do you have a lot of brothers and sisters or none at all? Do you live with your mom and dad, just one parent, or another family member? Is a family member home after school, or are you alone a lot? All of these things influence who you are and how you react to things.

When Characters (and People) Do Puzzling Things

Imagine a movie actor playing a superhero character. Most of the time, this superhero acts bravely and rushes to help those in need. But at one point in the movie, the superhero knows someone needs help and doesn't go to the rescue.

Why would she do that? The actor figures this out by putting herself in the superhero's shoes. She thinks, "If I were this superhero, why wouldn't I help this person?" Was there some event that happened—either recently or in her past—that influenced the superhero's thoughts and feelings about this mission? What were the superhero's beliefs about the situation? The actor may discover that the superhero recently tried to rescue someone but wasn't able to get there in time. Since then, she has been beating herself up about it. She might think she is a failure and doubt her ability to help people in the future. Therefore she didn't try to rescue the person in need because she was thinking she wouldn't be able to do it. Knowing this, the actor has much more sympathy for the character.

In real life, people also sometimes do and say things that we don't understand. Have you ever been yelled at before and wondered why? If you meet someone who doesn't act very nice or makes you upset, try asking yourself, "I wonder what it's like to walk in that person's shoes." Was this person having a bad day? Is he or she upset because of a family problem?

Similarly, we may sometimes do things that are out of character for us—things that other people would only understand if they saw the world from our perspective. For example, if you don't get enough sleep and someone at school tries to talk to you before your first class, you may snap at them and act kind of mean. They didn't do anything wrong. You got angry because you were overtired. If your friends don't know you are tired, they might be really upset. But, if you tell them you hadn't gotten enough sleep, they will probably be empathetic because they've been tired before, too.

96 * HOW TO FEEL GOOD

Ok, I've Switched Shoes . . . Now What?

After you switch shoes, you are left with a better understanding of why another person believed, said, or did what they did.
So, what should you do with that knowledge?

Reframe. Remember, reframing means that you find a more
helpful way of looking at a situation. Let's say your sister yelled
at you and made you upset. Before switching shoes, you
thought, "My sister is mean, and I am never going to forgive
her." After looking into it, you find out that, in school that day,
your sister was teased constantly by some girls in a higher
grade. So, after switching shoes, you look at the situation very
differently and think, "It's not OK that my sister took her
emotions out on me, but I know not to take it personally
because she was just really upset about being teased."

Consider saying something. Sometimes after we put ourselves
in another person's shoes, we realize we may have said or
done something hurtful, even if that wasn't our intention.
In that case, consider apologizing to the person by saying
something like, "I took some time to think about what
happened, and now I understand better what was going on.
I'm sorry if what I said upset you."

Other times, we may switch shoes with someone who said
or did something that upset us. If we discover we can relate to
some of the things they are going through, we may develop
empathy and compassion for them. In that case you may want
to tell them. Everyone wants to be understood, so telling
someone that you can relate to how they are feeling may make
them feel better. But, if that person is still having a tough time,
he or she may not be ready to talk to you about it. Plus, it's
important to remember that it is not your responsibility to fix
someone else's problems. If you find yourself feeling like you

are responsible for someone that way, the best thing to do is to discuss it with your parents, counselor, or teacher before saying anything.

Switch Shoes

A) Select a character from one of your favorite books or movies. Find a point in the story where the character did something that upset someone else. Put yourself in the character's shoes and try to understand that behavior. What was the character thinking and feeling? Did any past or present issues with friends or family influence the character's attitudes?

B) Think of a time when someone said or did something that upset you. Put yourself in his or her shoes. What might that person have been feeling or thinking? Could problems with friends, school, or family have played a role?

C) Think of a time when you said or did something to upset someone. Put yourself in that person's shoes. What do you think he or she was thinking and feeling? Can you see things from another perspective?

Discuss parts A, B, and C with a parent, teacher, or counselor.

Take on an Acting Role

Get together with one or more friends and play an acting game. Below are two acting scenes. Decide which role you will play. Before you start, think about the character you are playing. What might this character's attitudes toward other

> **If we discover we can relate to some of the things another person is going through, we may develop empathy and compassion for them.**

people be like? What about his beliefs about himself? Would he be optimistic and resilient? Easily frustrated?

SCENE I

Character I: Martha

Martha is 15. She has no brothers or sisters. Her mom has been fighting an illness for several years. This morning, Martha's dad had to take her mom to the hospital for treatment.

Character 2: Alex

Alex is also 15. His parents are divorced and he lives with his mom. He has an 8-year-old sister with severe asthma. She has a lot of trouble breathing sometimes and has to see the doctor frequently. Alex has to give a lot of extra help to his mom since his sister is sick.

Situation: Alex and Martha are in the same science class. Their teacher makes them lab partners. Martha doesn't want to work on the lab assignment. She sits at the desk and hardly says a word to Alex. Alex doesn't think it's fair that he should have to do the work all by himself, so they get into an argument and get in trouble with the teacher.

For discussion: Putting yourself in Alex and Martha's shoes, what do you think each of them was thinking and feeling? How do their family situations affect what they think and feel?

What do Alex and Martha have in common that could help them have empathy toward one another?

SCENE 2

Character 1: Shane

Shane is 13. He is a little bit overweight and has had a hard time making friends. This morning, his classmate called him a name in the hallway. Shane got very upset and went over to the corner of the lunchroom and sat by himself.

Character 2: Taylor

Taylor is 14. She just moved here with her parents, so this is her first year in this school. She has made one friend so far, but most of the other kids don't talk to her when she tries to join in their activities. She knows that adjusting to a new school can take time, so she reminds herself every day to just hang in there. She is optimistic she'll make good friends soon.

Situation: Taylor sees Shane sitting by himself in the lunchroom, looking upset. She goes over and asks him what's wrong. He explains that he was teased. She tells him she is new to the school and asks him if he'd like to sit down with her for lunch.

For discussion: Putting yourself in Shane and Taylor's shoes, what do you think each of them was thinking and feeling? How do their individual personal or family situations affect what they think and feel? What do Shane and Taylor have in common that helps them have sympathy or empathy toward one another?

Feel Sympathy and Empathy, and Act Compassionately

When we have sympathy or empathy toward others, we are more likely to act in kind and compassionate ways. Below are two examples of how you might act kindly toward someone else. Think of at least two more examples of your own. They could be times when you were concerned for someone and acted kindly, or when someone acted kindly toward you.

EXAMPLE 1

Feeling: Adam notices his soccer teammate is getting frustrated because he's having trouble throwing the ball in from the sideline. Adam used to have a hard time with throw-ins, too, so he knows how aggravating that can be.

Act of kindness: After practice, Adam offers to help his teammate work on his throw-ins.

EXAMPLE 2

Feeling: Amanda's friend Gretchen is very upset because her cat recently died. Though Amanda doesn't have any pets of her own, she has sympathy for Gretchen's loss.

Act of kindness: Amanda made a sympathy card and brought Gretchen one of her favorite treats—chocolate chip cookies.

SPRING BACK

You are like a spring. When you make a mistake or don't succeed at something the first time around, or when serious events like the death of a pet or loved one occur, it can stretch you to your limits until you think you're about to break. But you won't break, because humans are built to make mistakes.

Bouncing back over and over again from difficult events is called *resilience*. Being resilient means being strong. It means that, even though you know it may be tough and require hard work, you are committed to doing your best to cope with and overcome the tough times you experience in life.

How to Be Resilient

People use many different strategies for bouncing back. There's no single way to be resilient. But there are a lot of skills and traits resilient people share that help them overcome their problems.

First, they think positively about themselves and the future. They are optimistic. Being optimistic means being hopeful that things will turn out fine. Resilient people see difficult events as temporary setbacks rather than things that will throw them permanently off track. They also balance their optimism with realism. In other words, they aren't so optimistic that they don't see things clearly. For example, a person who is so optimistic that she thinks making straight As will be pretty easy is likely to have some setbacks. A resilient person will think positively that he's capable of getting straight As, but will also be realistic and understand that, to get those grades, he will have to put in a lot of effort.

The second characteristic resilient people have is that they are good friends with their emotions (just like we talked about in 5. *Make Friends With Your Feelings, [pg. 31]*). They recognize their emotions, know the situations or behaviors that resulted in their feeling that way, and they know what to do to make themselves feel better.

Third, although they are independent and take responsibility for their actions, resilient people also know how important it is to reach out to close friends, doctors, and counselors when they need help. Resilient people also tend to have a healthy perspective on life. Rather than getting down on themselves or seeing themselves as unlucky or helpless, they reframe difficult events as personal challenges designed to teach them something or make them stronger.

When we start blaming ourselves or others, we can sabotage our plan to bounce back.

It's important to understand that being resilient doesn't mean you don't get sad, embarrassed, or stressed when upsetting things happen. Being resilient means that you know how to cope with those emotions in a healthy way that makes you feel better. And because resilience can be learned, it's never too late to start bouncing back.

So, to be resilient, try to focus on these things:

* Thinking positively about yourself and boosting your self-esteem

* Being hopeful and optimistic about the future, while still keeping your expectations realistic

* Taking personal responsibility for mistakes you make without beating yourself up about them

* Coping with uncomfortable emotions, both independently and with the help of trusted other people

* Reframing traumatic events or mistakes as temporary setbacks that will help you grow

Things that Sabotage Springing Back

Resilient people believe in themselves. They know that they are better at some things than others. Rather than blaming themselves for their limitations, they look forward to working on challenges and developing their strengths. But believing in yourself can be challenging when things go wrong. And when we stop believing and start blaming ourselves or others, we can sabotage our plan to bounce back.

Here are a few things to watch out for in your quest to be resilient.

Pessimism. Pessimism is the opposite of optimism. Pessimistic people lack hope for the future. They believe that life will be one mistake or traumatic event after another, and they don't think it's very likely that they will succeed in bouncing back. Pessimists may also think that they don't have much control over what happens to them. That way of thinking makes them less likely to try to bounce back because they don't think anything they do will make a difference.

Catastrophizing. Catastrophizing means that, when we make a mistake or are faced with a difficult situation, we automatically think the worst. We blow the situation out of proportion and believe things are or will soon become a whole lot worse. For example, if you don't do very well on one test and then start to worry that you will do badly on the rest of your tests and maybe not pass a class, then you're catastrophizing. And when you make your problems seem that big, you make it much harder to bounce back.

Negative self-talk. We all have an inner voice. When our inner voice keeps repeating things about us that aren't nice or helpful, that's called negative self-talk. Has your inner voice ever said anything like this?

* "I'm not good at anything."
* "I'm not smart enough."
* "I'm not loveable."
* "I know I'm going to mess this up."
* "Everything's always my fault."

Negative self-talk can take a toll on your self-esteem and keep you from believing in yourself. And you have to believe in yourself to be resilient.

The Resilient Pianist

Andrew has been playing the piano for one year. At a recent recital, he forgot some notes, got his fingers all tangled, and had to start over a couple of times. When he was done playing, he was really embarrassed. He was also anxious because he was worried his parents would be mad at him.

When Andrew went home, he went straight to his room. At first, he felt like he didn't really want to talk to anyone. He started thinking some pretty negative things about himself. "I will never be good enough at the piano. I don't know why I bother," he thought. But he knew that kind of thinking wasn't helpful. So, to get his mind to stop being so negative, he said, "Stop!" And then he fought back: "I am pretty good at the piano," he thought. "I just didn't practice enough." He was honest with himself and admitted that he probably messed up because he decided not to practice 30 minutes each day, as his teacher had suggested. He went out of his room to see his parents. He told them he was upset, and they gave him a hug. He admitted to them that he should have practiced harder. They told him not to worry about messing up—in fact, they said it sounded like he learned something really important as a result. Andrew made a commitment to himself to begin practicing every day. He was hopeful that, if he stuck to the plan, he would do much better at the next recital.

Andrew took responsibility for his actions by owning up to not practicing enough. But, he chose not to beat himself up about it. He looked at the situation as a lesson that he had to learn so that he could get himself back on track. Like Andrew, you'll bounce back more quickly if you put an end to the negative self-talk and come up with a plan to move forward.

Conquer the Negative

To be resilient, it is important to work on changing your catastrophic, pessimistic, and otherwise negative thoughts. First, you have to identify them. To do that, keep a journal. Every time you face a difficult challenge, take a moment to observe what you're thinking and write it down in your journal. When you find negative thoughts, use some of the strategies we talked about in *1. Have a Positive Attitude (pg. 9)* to dispute them. Ask yourself: "Is this belief logical, or am I just thinking this because I'm upset?," "Do I have any proof that this is true?," and, "Is this thought useful?" You can also reframe the thoughts. Is there a more useful way you could look at the situation so that it is more positive and hopeful?

Think Ahead

It is important to be hopeful, but it's also important to have realistic expectations about the future. Hard as we try, we cannot avoid making mistakes or suffering personal losses. This is a normal part of being human. You can, however, prepare yourself for the possibility that some situations might not go as planned. For example, before his recital, Andrew the pianist could have mentally prepared himself for the possibility that he might make a mistake. In his mind, he could imagine himself getting his fingers tangled. What should he do? Start over from the beginning? Just keep playing from the spot where he messed up? And, after the recital, how should he handle it if someone comments on his mistake? Should he laugh it off and say, "Yeah, I wish I hadn't messed up, but I'll do better next time"? Should he admit that he should have practiced harder? And how will he cope with being embarrassed and upset with himself? Should he go home and deal with it by himself, or talk about with his parents?

Don't expect mistakes to happen, but planning for mistakes can make you more self-confident and help you spring back more quickly.

Feel Good About Yourself

Develop your strengths. Feeling like we're really good at something makes us more confident in ourselves, and self-confidence is key to springing back. Pick something you are good at—writing, cooking, singing, or sports, for example—and work even harder at it than you already do. Make a schedule to practice it a little bit each day.

Take On New Responsibilities

Taking on new responsibilities puts you in charge of something important and gives you the opportunity to prove to yourself how capable you are. By volunteering to be in charge of something, you get to make important decisions. This can be empowering and boost your self-esteem. It's best to start off volunteering to do something you know you can handle. For example, you could volunteer to water the plants at home or at school every day or to feed the family dog his dinner every evening.

Find a Role Model

Do some research to find examples of people who have overcome adversity. Ask for guidance from a parent, teacher, or counselor. What did this person do to overcome his or her difficulties? Think of some positive thoughts this person may have had in order to persevere. Come up with some ideas for how you might do the same thing in your life.

CHOOSE WHERE YOU WANT TO GO

What do you want to do when you get older? Do you dream every day about the things you could do? Do you choose to work on things that will help you reach your dreams, or do you sit back and wait for something fun and new to come your way? Do you ever look back at the things you have done to see just how much you have accomplished?

Life is like a flowing river that carries you along its waters. If you wanted to, you could let the current carry you from place to place. The river and its rocks and fish would choose your direction for you, bouncing you from shore to shore. If you sit back and let the river decide your course, you could end up lost and out of control on raging rapids or bored, stuck in a trickling stream that doesn't move at your pace.

Instead of letting life happen to you, you can choose to use your oars and steer yourself where you want to go. How do you do that?

Visualize Where You Want to Go

If you don't see yourself being successful at something, you will be less likely to take active steps to get there. *Creative visualization*—sometimes called *guided mental imagery*—is a technique that involves using your imagination to create a mental picture in your head. Once you decide on a goal—say, to play a C Major chord on the guitar—you close your eyes, take a few deep breaths, and imagine yourself sitting on a stool with the guitar in your hands. Feel the guitar strap around your shoulder and back while you hold the neck of the guitar in one hand and the guitar pick in the other. Position your fingers on the correct strings. Really press down and feel the smooth strings beneath your fingertips. Notice what your hand feels like. It probably feels really awkward at first, so reposition it so that it starts to feel more natural. Now, before you play it, imagine the sound of the C major chord. That's what it's going to sound like when you strum the strings with your guitar pick. Now, strum. Feel the strings vibrate. Hear the solid sound come from the guitar. Feel proud of what you did. Strum again.

Visualization can boost your confidence and improve your mental awareness. *Repeated mental rehearsal*—that is, mentally visualizing success over and over again on a regular basis—can also help keep you motivated and focused on your goal.

Set SMART Goals

SMART is an acronym. Each letter in SMART is the first letter of another word. And all those words together describe the best way to set goals.

S stands for specific. Goals should be specific, clear, and detailed. For example, what does it mean if you say, "I'm going to get good grades on my next report card"? How do you define "good grades"? Is that the same as how your parents or your teacher define "good grades"? Be more specific to clear up any confusion and give you a clearer target to aim for. Say, "I am going to get a B or better in math and all As in the rest of my classes on my next report card."

M stands for measurable. To know whether or not you've succeeded, you must be able to actually measure your goals. For example, let's say this was your goal: "I'm going to get less frustrated at soccer practice." How do you measure "less frustrated"? Instead, why not modify this goal to say that every time you are frustrated during soccer practice, you will take a short break to say to yourself, "Soccer drills can be frustrating, but I know I can handle it," and, "I don't have to do the drills perfectly. Learning from my mistakes helps me get better." That goal is measurable. After practice, you will be able to say you either did achieve your goal or you didn't.

M can also stand for *meaningful* and *motivational.* Your goal should be important to you and it should inspire you to want to achieve it. In other words, set goals that you truly care about.

A stands for attainable. Your goal should be realistic. It should challenge you to work hard, but not be so difficult that it's unlikely you'll be able to achieve it. **A** also stands for *agreed-upon.* If your goal involves other people—friends, teachers, or parents, for example—you should let them know about your goal and make sure they agree to participate. For example, you would want to be sure that your soccer coach knows about your plans to take a short break to deal with your frustration.

R stands for relevant. That just means that your goals should fit your interests and be appropriate for your age. Goals should be personal and appropriate for *you*. **R** also stands for *realistic*. Set yourself up for success by setting goals you can reach. It's OK to aim high, but when you expect too much of yourself, you're not being realistic and that just sets you up to fail. Your goal should be something you can do within a reasonable amount of time with the resources you have. For example, if you only have access to a swimming pool twice a week, it wouldn't be realistic to set a goal of improving your 100 meter swim time by 30 seconds in one week. That doesn't give you enough of an opportunity to practice and get faster.

Also, make sure to consider other time commitments when making your goals. If you are already busy with school, sports, and other activities, setting a goal that requires you to spend two hours a day working on a special project may lead you to get frustrated with yourself because you can't possibly carve out that kind of time. Instead, start smaller. Try setting a goal to work on that special project for 15 minutes each day. If you meet that goal with ease, then you can think about setting your goal higher.

T stands for time-bound. When you set a goal, it is important to establish a time limit. Setting a time limit can be tricky. The time frame should be short enough to challenge you, but if it's too short, you may get frustrated. On the other hand, setting a time limit that is too long may fail to motivate you. For example, you could set a goal to read one book per day, per week,

Visualization can boost your confidence and improve your mental awareness.

per month, or per school semester. Which time frame is realistic, but also short enough to challenge and motivate you?

Look Back to Check Your Progress

Looking back at your progress to see how far you've come is an important step in building your confidence and giving you the encouragement you need to keep going. You might think you're not making any progress at all because it can take time to work your way toward your long-term goals. But if you track your goals every week, you will see that you are actually a long way from where you first started. You will be more confident in yourself when you take charge of where you are headed in life.

Set a SMART Goal

Write down one goal you want to accomplish this week. Work with a parent, teacher, or counselor to help make it a SMART goal—specific, measurable, attainable, realistic, and time-bound. Next, write down a plan for how you will reach your goal. At the end of the time period you established, discuss whether you met your goal. If you didn't, figure out what you could do differently next time. Was the goal unrealistic? Or did unhelpful thoughts get in the way of your being successful?

Use Creative Visualization

Use guided mental imagery to help you successfully reach your SMART goal. Sit in a quiet place with your eyes closed. Imagine yourself doing everything you need to do to accomplish what you want. Remember to use all of your senses. Visualize success every day until you reach your goal.

Track Your Progress

On a chalkboard or dry erase board, make a chart. In one column, list all of your past and present goals. In another column, write down whether you accomplished the goal or are still working toward it. Look at the chart daily to remind yourself how much you've accomplished and to motivate yourself to keep working hard.

COMFORT YOURSELF

Have you ever been stressed out? You have a test tomorrow at school, your brother won't stop bugging you, your mom is telling you to pick up your room and someone who you thought was your friend now always picks on you and you just can't figure out why. Sometimes it just all seems like so much to handle.

What do you do when you are stressed out? Do you head for the refrigerator and grab a snack? Get grouchy and snap at people? Talk to a friend or family member about it? Go outside for a walk or to play?

People handle stress in all kinds of ways. Some ways are helpful because they calm us down and help us remember that we can handle anything that comes our way. Other ways are not so helpful because they may not keep us from feeling badly or reacting *impulsively* (without thinking).

You can feel better by choosing useful ways of dealing with stress. Managing your emotions effectively, on your own, is called *self-soothing* or *emotional self-regulation*. Self-regulation means that you are able to tolerate difficult emotions and control how you react to them. Here are some ways you can practice managing your emotions.

Identifying What You're Feeling

We talked a lot in 5. *Make Friends With Your Feelings (pg. 31)* about how important it is to get to know your emotions. The earlier you can recognize what you feel, the earlier you can take action to soothe it. If we're not paying attention, we may not notice something is wrong until those feelings have gotten so strong that it's hard to get control of them. So, even if you don't know the exact name of the emotion, just becoming aware that you're feeling something unpleasant is enough to let you know it's time to act.

Picking a Self-Soothing Tool From Your Tool Belt

The good news is, there are a lot of different ways to cope with emotions that come on suddenly, that are really uncomfortable, or that seem overwhelming. Think of each of these techniques as a different tool that you can keep in your tool belt. You can pull one or more of them out whenever you need to.

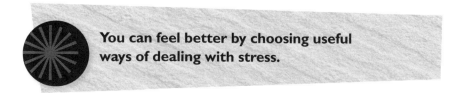

You can feel better by choosing useful ways of dealing with stress.

Tool 1: The hammer. Challenge your negative inner voice. Your inner voice reflects your thoughts and beliefs about yourself and the situations you face. If you repeatedly think things like, "There's no way I can handle this," you may be more likely to feel really stressed or upset, and that can lead you to believe that you aren't capable of coping on your own. Just as it's important to learn to recognize your emotions, it's also important to learn to recognize your inner thoughts so that you can address them before they worsen your emotions or affect your self-esteem.

Once you've identified these negative beliefs, dispute them. Hammer them out! Talk back to your inner voice and explain why those thoughts aren't useful or logical. Strengthen the case against that negative inner voice by providing evidence that those beliefs are wrong. For example, you might say, "Actually, I made it through a stressful situation in the past, so that means I'm capable of doing it again." Adjust your expectations if necessary. For example, is your inner voice telling you that you that it's never acceptable to feel really sad or angry? Remind yourself that emotions—even difficult ones—are normal and tend to come and go, so there's nothing wrong with you for feeling upset when faced with a challenging situation. For more examples of how to successfully challenge your inner voice, refer to *1. Have a Positive Attitude (pg. 9).*

Tool 2: The screwdriver. Even if you're in the middle of class and unable to leave, you can always calm yourself down by tightening the screws. Practice breathing or visualization. Inhale deeply through your nose. Breathe from your belly so that when you inhale, your stomach moves outward. Then exhale deeply through your nose, bringing your stomach back in. Keep doing that as long as you need to until you feel yourself becoming calmer. You may also find it helpful to visualize something pleasant. Create a mental picture of something that makes you feel good. For example, imagine yourself running on the beach. Feel the wet sand between your toes. See the ocean waves coming into shore. Visualize walking into the water so that it comes up to your ankles. Is the water cold? Can you feel seaweed touch your toes or ankles?

Tool 3: The measuring tape. Take a time-out. Sometimes it is helpful to measure out the time. Some people think of time-outs as punishment. But taking your own time-out isn't punishment at all—it's a positive way to give yourself a break from a situation that is challenging for you to handle. When you can, walk away from the situation for five or ten minutes. Go someplace quiet and sit down. You may even want to create a special place in your room at home that makes you feel safe and comfortable. Put your favorite pillow, blanket, or stuffed animal there to soothe you. While you're in the time-out, breathe slowly and deeply and visualize something that makes you happy, like being on the beach, playing your favorite game, or running on a soccer field. If unhelpful thoughts keep coming into your mind, just let them pass and repeat positive thoughts like, "This situation is frustrating, but I know I can handle it."

Tool 4: The drill. Get some exercise. Physical activity can help us drill down and get to trapped feelings of anger or anxiety. And, if we're sad, getting up and moving can improve our mood and our attitude. Riding your bike, taking a walk, jumping rope, or skateboarding are all healthy ways to clear out our minds and soothe our emotions.

Tool 5: The pliers. When you're feeling bent out of shape, doing something relaxing can be a good way to bend you back to where you feel comfortable. There are a lot of different ways to relax. Listening to music, playing with your pet, or reading are great examples. But be careful—some things that relax you aren't necessarily very healthy for you. For example, some people like to eat when they get stressed out. But eating the unhealthy things, or eating for the wrong reasons (because you're stressed out instead of actually being hungry), may make you feel better temporarily, but not for long.

Tool 6: The wrench. Know when to ask for help. Sometimes you can't unstick a sticky situation with just your own two hands—and that's fine. Emotions can seem overwhelming, and self-soothing sometimes isn't enough to make us feel better. Knowing when to ask for help from someone you trust, like your parents or a teacher or school counselor, is just as important as knowing how to self-regulate. Don't let unhelpful thoughts like, "Smart and strong kids don't ask for help," discourage you. Remember, we all need help sometimes, so don't be afraid to use this tool when you need it.

Recognize the Signs

How do you know you need comforting? What do you feel in your body when you get upset? Does your stomach hurt? Does your heart race? Do your muscles get tight? Does your face scrunch up? Make a list of all the signs you can think of that let you know you need to do something to comfort yourself. Carry that list with you in your pocket. For one week, monitor your symptoms. Every time you feel one of those signs, write down the day and time you felt it, and what was going on at the time. Show this list to your parents, teacher, or counselor and talk about how you can handle those situations. Below are some examples.

Sign	Day and time	What was happening
Stomach hurts	Monday, 9:30 a.m.	Pop quiz in school
Pressure in my head	Wednesday, 12 p.m.	Classmate stole part of my lunch

Anticipate

Some situations may be more difficult to handle than others. For example, maybe you have a hard time dealing with change, so whenever a new school year begins and you change teachers or schools, you feel a lot of anxiety and have a hard time soothing yourself. You may be more successful in regulating those unhelpful feelings if you're prepared for them. *Anticipating,* or looking ahead to identify situations that may create difficult emotions, can give you the chance to make a plan for what to do. Think of a situation that gets you really upset. Work with a parent, teacher, or counselor to help prepare yourself for that event.

Find Healthy Ways to Comfort Yourself

Below is a list of some things kids might do when they're upset and want to feel better. Some of these things are healthy ways to cope, but others aren't so good for you. Take note of the ones you did this week. Are there any others you can think of to add to the list? If you used any of the unhealthy ones, decide which healthy activity you could use to replace the bad one. Try out your new healthy coping skills this week, and keep a journal of how it feels when you comfort yourself in healthy ways.

Unhealthy: Hit or hurt yourself; eat; lose your temper; pretend nothing's wrong (try to forget about it); take it out on someone else (yelling or teasing).

Healthy: Talk to your parents, teachers, or loved ones; play or be active; draw or write in a journal; listen to music; pet your dog; try to think of a solution to the problem; meditate or engage in creative visualization; do deep breathing exercises.

APPRECIATE THE VALUE OF YOUR HARD WORK

Have you ever done something you thought was really great, but it seemed like nobody else even noticed? Maybe you finished reading a book for school, or helped a classmate understand something, or tried a new vegetable without anybody even telling you to, and nobody was there to give you a hug, a pat on the back, or to say, "Good job."

Sometimes when nobody is there to recognize things we do, we think that maybe what we did wasn't so special after all. And if what we did wasn't special or important, we may think we're not so special or important either. We may be pessimistic and engage in *negative self-talk* (there's more on this in *17. Spring Back [pg. 101]*), thinking things like, "What I do doesn't make a difference," or, "I'm never going to be good enough."

The truth is, people do care. It's just that they sometimes get busy or forget to tell you how important your hard work is or how proud they are of you. And your hard work not only matters to others, it matters to you. You wouldn't choose to work hard at something unless it was important to you, right? Hard work can help you learn and give you an opportunity to help others. It can also allow you to express your creativity and show you just what you are capable of. Even if nobody ever said, "thank you," or, "good job," or if you never got an award or top grade, that wouldn't take away the most important reward of all—how much that hard work helps you grow.

Self-Reward

To stay motivated and be resilient, it is important to learn how to *self-reward*. That means you recognize and praise yourself for your efforts and achievements. So, how do you do that?

First, be mindful. That means paying close attention to what is going on in the present. Take some quiet time to yourself to look at the project you finished, the thing you helped build, the nice deed that you did, or the art you created. Look at what you can do when you set your mind to something. Realize how good it feels to know that you are capable of finishing something all on your own or by working with others. Feel the excitement of knowing that, if you did it once, you can surely do it again. Notice that your hard work brings great results. You will probably find that the positive feelings and awareness of your strengths that mindfulness brings are big rewards all by themselves.

The truth is, people do care. It's just that they sometimes get busy or forget to tell you how important your hard work is or how proud they are of you.

Second, pat yourself on the back in a way that's meaningful to you. Something that is a reward to one person may not be rewarding for another. So think of something you could do for yourself in recognition of your hard work. If you love reading, you could reward yourself by checking out a new book at the library to read in your spare time. If you like music, you could reward yourself by listening to your music collection for 30 minutes after school or before bed. What else do you enjoy that would be rewarding for you? Cooking? Watching movies?

You don't have to do a task perfectly to earn praise. Sometimes just attempting an activity at all can be a really big step. For example, maybe you are shy and anxious around other kids and usually eat your lunch alone. One day you decide to take a chance and go sit down at a table with some classmates. That was a really big deal to you because you weren't sure whether they would tell you to leave or welcome you to their table. Even if other kids say unhelpful things about what you've done, or if your parents or teachers aren't there to support you, it's important to remain confident in the value of your hard work. Maybe you never said a word at the table even though you wanted to join in the conversation, but that's ok. You took a very important step by just going over to them. You could set a goal to participate in the conversation the next day at the lunch table.

Staying Motivated

When you get frustrated and your inner voice says, "Well, if nobody cares, then why am I bothering to put in all this hard work?" try challenging that negative thought. One way to do that is to prove that what you did actually does matter. Think about why it's important to you or others in the long-term.

For example, why was it important to take a seat at the lunch table? If you never took that risk, you would continue to be shy and anxious. Try *reframing* the situation. Instead of thinking that no one values your hard work, look at your experience as an opportunity to practice self-reward. Remind yourself that we all need to learn how to praise ourselves if we're going to be resilient and persevere in life. This is a valuable opportunity for you to learn how to give yourself credit.

Pride and Responsibility

Working hard and taking responsibility for things is really important for building your self-esteem. That's why, even when you don't get the recognition you would like for the hard work you do, it is important not to give up. Taking pride in what you do means that you get a sense of satisfaction from it. It makes you feel good to put a lot of care and effort into the things you do. Believing in yourself enough to take responsibility for new tasks puts you in charge of something important. It gives you the opportunity to prove to yourself how capable you are. By volunteering to be in charge of something, you get to make important decisions, and this can empower you. You may discover that it feels so good to be hard-working and dedicated enough to manage responsibilities on your own that you no longer focus on getting praise from others.

Start a System of Self-Reward

Sometimes it can be a drag to do the everyday work we have to do. Our parents sometimes have to nag us to do things like homework, cleaning our rooms, and brushing our teeth. But if you took charge and decided to do those things without anyone telling you to, you might start to feel really good about yourself. On a piece of paper or chalkboard, make a chart. In one column, list activities you sometimes don't want to do because they're not always much fun and they're a lot of work. Then list each day of the week in the separate columns. Every time you take responsibility for that task and do it without being asked, put a star, sticker, or other mark on the chart and reward yourself! You decide how you want to reward yourself—you could be mindful and tune in to the good feeling of doing something on your own or you could treat yourself to a new book or watching a movie.

Write Yourself Some Words of Encouragement

Write a letter to yourself. In the letter, tell yourself how proud you are of the hard work you just did. Remind yourself that taking pride in what you do will help you be resilient and reach your long-term goals. Fold up the letter and keep it in your pocket or backpack. Every time you do something helpful for yourself or others, pull out the letter and read it. Take a few moments to smile and notice how it feels to be kind and supportive to yourself.

Be Mindful of Your Hard Work

Sometimes we develop a habit of downplaying our hard work. We might say some of the great things we do are "no big deal," or, "not important." But not giving yourself credit for helping yourself or other people can lead to you develop unrealistic standards and expectations. List three things you're proud of doing this week. What positive impact did these things have on you or others?

ABOUT THE AUTHOR

Tricia Mangan has a Master's degree in Clinical Psychology from Stony Brook University. She has more than 10 years of diverse clinical, research, and teaching experience. With a background rooted in cognitive-behavioral and positive psychology principles, Tricia is a proponent of a holistic approach to health and is currently focusing her efforts on writing books to educate children and teens on the mind-body connection.

ABOUT
MAGINATION PRESS

Magination Press publishes self-help books for kids and the adults in their lives. Magination Press in an imprint of the American Psychological Association, the largest scientific and professional organization representing psychologists in the United States and the largest association of psychologists worldwide.